HISTORIC
Parks and Gardens
in and around
South Yorkshire

Joan + Neil Jone

Crucible Teemer outside Sheffield Town Hall.

Herbaceous Border, Renishaw Hall Garden.

Winter Garden, Sheffield.

Glasshouse, Cannon Hall.

HISTORIC
Parks and Gardens
in and around
South Yorkshire

Joan & Mel Jones

First published in Great Britain in 2005 by
WHARNCLIFFE BOOKS
an imprint of
Pen & Sword Books Limited
47 Church Street
Barnsley
South Yorkshire
S70 2AS

Copyright © Joan & Mel Jones

ISBN 1 903425 47 6

The right of Joan and Mel Jones to be
identified as Authors of this Work has
been asserted by them in accordance with the
Copyright, Designs and Patents Act 1988.

A CIP catalogue record for this book
is available from the British Library.

Printed and bound in Singapore by
Kyodo Printing Co. (Singapore) Pte Ltd

Pen & Sword Books Ltd incorporates the imprints of
Pen & Sword Aviation, Pen & Sword Maritime, Pen & Sword Military,
Wharncliffe Books, Pen & Sword Select,
Pen & Sword Military Classics and Leo Cooper.

For a complete list of Pen & Sword titles please contact:
PEN & SWORD BOOKS LIMITED
47 Church Street, Barnsley, South Yorkshire, S70 2AS, England.
E-mail: enquiries@pen-and-sword.co.uk
Website: www.pen-and-sword.co.uk

CONTENTS

INTRODUCTION · 6

1. PARKS · 7

2. THE ENGLISH ORNAMENTAL GARDEN · · · · · · · · · · · · · · · · 27

3. THE COUNTRY HOUSE KITCHEN GARDEN · · · · · · · · · · · · · · 39

4. VISITOR GUIDE

Barnsley's Urban Public Parks:
    Locke Park · 51
Brodsworth Hall Gardens · 54
Cannon Hall, Park and Gardens · · · · · · · · · · · · · · · · · · · 57
Clumber Park and Walled Kitchen Garden · · · · · · · · · · · · · 63
Cusworth Hall and Park · 67
Doncaster's Urban Public Parks:
    Elmfield Park · 72
    Hexthorpe Flatts · 72
Fanshawe Gate Hall and Gardens · · · · · · · · · · · · · · · · · 74
Hodsock Priory Gardens · 76
Nostell Priory Park, Pleasure Grounds and Gardens · · · · · · · 79
Renishaw Hall Garden and Park · · · · · · · · · · · · · · · · · · · 83
Rotherham's Urban Public Parks:
    Boston Castle and Park · · · · · · · · · · · · · · · · · · · 86
    Clifton Park · 90
Sheffield Botanical Gardens · 94
Sheffield's Urban Public Parks:
    Firth Park · 101
    Hillsborough Park · 105
    Limb Valley (Whinfell Quarry Gardens, Whirlow Brook Park) · · · 108
    Meersbrook Park · 110
    Norfolk Park · 112
    Porter Valley (Endcliffe Park, Bingham Park, Whiteley Woods,
       Porter Clough) · 114
    Weston Park · 118
Wentworth Castle and Stainborough Park and Gardens · · · · · · 121
Wentworth Woodhouse, Park and Gardens · · · · · · · · · · · · 130
Wortley Hall, Park and Gardens · · · · · · · · · · · · · · · · · · · 138
Yorkshire Sculpture Park, West Bretton · · · · · · · · · · · · · · · 145

NOTES AND REFERENCES · 148
INDEX · 157

$\mathcal{I}$NTRODUCTION

We hope readers have as much pleasure in reading this book and visiting and exploring the historic parks and gardens included in it as we have had in compiling it. We have combined research in libraries and archives with prolonged visits to all the sites at all times of the year. And what a pleasure that has been, beginning with Hodsock on bright February days and ending with walks through the park at Wentworth or round the garden at Wortley Hall on crisp late December days.

The book is organised quite simply. The first three chapters deal respectively with the history of parks (deer parks, landscaped parks and public parks), ornamental gardens and kitchen gardens, with a view to putting local parks and gardens into their national historical context. These are followed by site-by-site guides to nearly thirty parks and gardens throughout South Yorkshire and just across the boundary in neighbouring West Yorkshire, north Derbyshire and north Nottinghamshire.

The book could not have been compiled without the help of a number of key individuals and organisations who have given us their valuable time and in a number of cases useful illustrative material. We would particularly like to thank Geoff Albiston; Pauline and Michael Bentley; Steve Blackbourn of Clifton Park Museum; Jean Brown; Lynn Dunning of Cannon Hall Museum; Richard Evans of Wentworth Castle and Stainborough Park Heritage Trust; Jane Furse; Phil Gill of Rotherham MBC; Julie Harrup of Cusworth Hall; Ken Hawley and Christine Ball of the Hawley Collection Trust; Catherine Higham; Marc Mallender, Head Gardener at Wortley Hall; Chris Margrave, Head Gardener at Wentworth Castle; Darrell Maryon of Heeley City Farm; Ian Mitchell and Liz Neild-Banks of Sheffield City Council; Neil Porteous, Head Gardener at Clumber Park kitchen garden; Joan Sewell for her detailed report on Sheffield's public parks; Paul Varney of Barnsley MBC; Gareth Williams of the National Trust at Nostell Priory; Arroll Winning; Janet Worrall, Secretary of the Friends of Boston Castle; and last but not least the staff in the Archives and Local Studies Libraries at Barnsley, Doncaster, Rotherham and Sheffield.

Acknowledgements are due to the Head of Leisure Services, Sheffield City Council, and the following individuals or organisations for permission to quote from their collections in Sheffield Archives: S W Fraser Esq. (Spencer Stanhope Muniments); Major C J Vernon Wentworth (Vernon-Wentworth Muniments) and the Milton (Peterborough) Estates Company (Wentworth Woodhouse Muniments). We also wish to acknowledge permission from the Head of Leisure Services and the Trustees of the Wharncliffe Estates to quote from and reproduce an illustration (WhM 147/19) in the Wharncliffe Muniments also in Sheffield Archives. We also wish to thank the Hunter Archaeological Society for permission to reproduce a sketch (HAS 81) from a letter in their Gatty collection in Sheffield Archives. Thanks are also due to Doncaster Archives for allowing access to the Battie-Wrightson of Cusworth collection. Detailed references to the sources of quotations from documents in the various archive collections are given in the Notes and References section at the end of the book. We would also like to thank Anthea Greaves for her botanical illustrations and Eric Leslie for his ink and wash drawings. All the modern photographs are by the authors.

$\mathscr{P}$ARKS

$\mathscr{P}$arks are as old as civilisation itself. They originated in ancient Assyria, Persia, India, Egypt, Greece and Rome. More than 3,000 years ago the king of Assyria boasted of parks planted with exotic trees, stocked with oxen, stags and elephants, embellished with fish ponds and beautified with complex water systems and with temples and shrines on artificially created small hills.

Deer parks

The first parks in Britain were deer parks. The concept of the deer park is probably of Roman origin but although they certainly existed in England in Saxon times they were few and far between, and the tradition only flourished after the Norman Conquest of 1066. In the Domesday Survey of 1086, twenty years after the Conquest, only thirty-five deer parks were recorded. Estimates of the number of deer parks in existence in England by the year 1300 vary – one authority suggests 1,900,[1] another puts the figure at over 3,000.[2]

Medieval deer parks were symbols of status and wealth. They were created by kings, by the nobility and by bishops, and they were also attached to monasteries, nunneries and colleges. As all deer were deemed to belong to the Crown, from the beginning of the thirteenth century it was necessary to obtain a licence from the king to create a park. This was called a right of free warren and it empowered the grantee

The essence of a deer park: a herd of deer in a laund with an ancient oak tree.

to kill deer and to preserve them by creating an enclosed deer park. The medieval parks at Conisbrough and Sheffield – now disappeared from the landscape except for place-names in the case of Conisbrough, and two important buildings (see below) in the case of Sheffield – predated the issuing of Royal licences and so must have been of twelfth century or even earlier, possibly Saxon, origin. Searches of parish histories, principally Hunter's two-volume *South Yorkshire*,[3] reveal that more than eighty grants of free warren were granted in the medieval period in South Yorkshire, and that at least 25 deer parks were created.[4]

Nationally the great age of park creation was the century and a half between 1200 and 1350, a period of growing population and agricultural prosperity. Landowners had surplus wealth and there were still sufficient areas of waste on which to create parks. In South Yorkshire the majority of grants of free warren were given in the period from 1250 to 1325 when forty-four grants were made. Significantly, no grants were given for thirty years following the Black Death (1349), but then there were twenty-one grants between 1379 and 1400. The last known medieval grant of free warren was in 1491-92 when Brian Sandford was granted permission to create a park at Thorpe Salvin. This grant is also notable for the fact that it was accompanied by a gift of twelve does from the king's park at Conisbrough 'towards the storing of his parc at Thorp'.[5] The last-known local grant of free warren was given to the 2nd Viscount Castleton in 1637 by King Charles I to create a deer park at Sandbeck. The licence (which is in Latin) says that Viscount Castleton was given permission to

> Make separate with pales, walls or hedges 500 acres or thereabouts of land, meadow, pasture, gorse, heath, wood, underwood, woodland tenements and hereditaments … to make a park where deer and other wild animals might be grazed and kept.[6]

Deer parks were still being created or re-stocked in South Yorkshire as late as the eighteenth century (see visitor guide to Cannon Hall).

Deer parks were not created primarily for hunting although hunting did take place in the larger parks. Besides their status symbol role their main function was to provide for their owners a reliable source of food for the table and supplies of wood and timber. They were, therefore, an integral part of the farming economy. The killing of deer for venison was often reserved for special occasions. A good local example was the funeral of the fifth Earl of Shrewsbury in 1560 when, for the great dinner held in Sheffield Castle following the funeral, fifty does (female fallow deer) and twenty-nine red deer were killed and cooked.[7]

The deer in most parks were fallow deer, which were not native to Britain and were probably introduced by the Normans. Fallow deer were much easier to contain within a park than the native red and roe deer. Locally both fallow and red deer were kept in parks. In John Harrison's Survey of the Manor of Sheffield in 1637, the park there was said to be 'not meanly furnished with fallow Deare, the number of them at present is one Thousand'.[8] Nearly a century later when Daniel Defoe rode through Tankersley Park he commented that he had seen 'the largest red deer that, I believe, are in this part of Europe. One of the hinds, I think, was larger than my horse...'[9] Besides deer, wild swine, hares, rabbits (also introduced by the Normans and kept in burrows in artificially made mounds) and game birds were kept in medieval parks. Herds of cattle and flocks of sheep were also grazed there. Another important feature of medieval deer parks were fish ponds to provide an alternative to meat in Lent and on fast days.

Although there are records of parks without trees, deer parks usually consisted of woodland and areas largely cleared of trees. The park livestock could graze in the open areas and find cover in the wooded areas. The cleared areas were called launds (from which the modern word *lawn* originates) or plains and consisted of grassland or heath with scattered trees. Most of the trees in the launds would have been pollarded, ie, trees cut at least six feet from the ground leaving a massive lower trunk called a bolling above which a continuous crop of new growth sprouted out of reach of the grazing deer, sheep and cattle. John Evelyn, in his book *Sylva*, first published in the second half of the seventeenth century, recorded some massive pollards in the deer park at Sheffield. For example he recorded one oak tree whose trunk was thirteen feet in diameter and another ten yards in circumference. In the launds regeneration of trees was restricted because of continual grazing and new trees were only able to grow in the protection of thickets of hawthorn and holly. Some of these unpollarded trees might reach a great age and size and were much sought after for major building projects. Evelyn recorded a large oak tree felled in Sheffield Park that was so big when lying on its side that two men on horseback on either side could not see each other's hats. Even more impressive was his report that in an open area within the park called Conduit Plaine there was another oak whose branches were so far spreading that he estimated (giving all his calculations) that 251 horses could stand in its shade.[10]

The woods within medieval deer parks were managed in different ways. Some woods were 'holted', ie, they consisted of single-stemmed trees grown for their timber like a modern plantation. Most woods were coppiced and were surrounded by a bank or wall to keep out the grazing animals during the early years of regrowth. Later in the coppice cycle the deer would have been allowed into the coppice woods. There were also separate woods or special compartments within coppice woods in which the dominant tree was holly and which were called holly hags. The holly was cut in winter

A veteran ash in Bretton Old Deer Park.

An extract from John Speed's map of the West Riding of Yorkshire, 1610, showing seven surviving medieval deer parks.

for the deer and other park livestock. In a lease of 1653 for Tankersley Park it was stipulated that the deer had to be fed in winter 'with holley to be cut therein.'[11]

Between the late fifteenth and eighteenth centuries many medieval deer parks either changed their function and hence their appearance, or disappeared altogether. John Speed's map of the West Riding of Yorkshire published in 1610 shows only nine surviving deer parks in South Yorkshire: at Wortley, Tankersley, Brierley, Sheffield, Kimberworth, Thrybergh, Conisbrough, Treeton and Aston. Only the outline of Tanksersley Park has survived to the present day in any recognisable form.

When a landlord was absent (his main country seat may have been in another parish or county) or where his hall lay some distance away from his medieval park, there was increased possibility that the park might disappear altogether, the process being called disparkment. Well-wooded parks often simply became large coppice woods. Other parks simply reverted to farmland.

While hundreds of medieval deer parks were disappearing, many others took on a new lease of life and many new parks were created because the concept of the park was changing. Its primary function changed from being a game preserve and a valuable source of wood and timber to being the adornment of a country house. New residences were built within existing parks and the park boundaries extended.

Landscaped parks

The concept of the park as an aesthetic extension of a country seat and its garden began in the Tudor period and has gone through a number of fashions during the last 500 years.

In the Tudor period in the sixteenth century three fundamental changes took place. First, with a stable and strong central government, major landowners in England gradually abandoned their fortified residences – their castles and moated manor houses – and began to build country houses. Secondly they built these in the middle of existing

The Turret House of Sheffield Manor located in the middle of Sheffield Deer Park.

deer parks or created completely new parks on new sites. Thirdly, they immediately surrounded their new country houses with formal gardens (see Chapter 2). The new fashion for locating a new country house in the centre of an existing deer park is well illustrated in South Yorkshire at Tankersley. There the moat of the former moated manor house still survives and surrounds the nineteenth century rectory to the north of the church, while in the centre of the former park lie the ruins of the Elizabethan Tankersley Hall. Even more substantial was the Manor Lodge built about 1510 on an eminence, with glorious views in every direction, in Sheffield Park by the 4th Earl of Shrewsbury and largely dismantled in the early eighteenth century. Now largely in ruins except for the Turret House (often erroneously said to have been the gaol of Mary, Queen of Scots, but more likely a banqueting house and look-out point over the surrounding park), it was described in his 1637 Survey of the Manor of Sheffield by John Harrison as

> Ye scite of Sheffield Lodge standing on a hill in ye middle of ye Parke being fairly built with stone & Timber with an Inward and an outward Court 2 Gardens & 3 Yards...[12]

There was a great transfer of property from monastic to lay ownership in the 1530s and 1540s which also resulted in the creation of new parks setting off grand new houses often incorporating the remains of abbeys, priories and nunneries. Locally, Nostell Priory in West Yorkshire occupies the site of an Augustinian priory.

The parks surrounding the new country houses that sprang up in the sixteenth and seventeenth centuries, were still essentially deer parks, although grazing cattle were a much more common sight than in the medieval period, with both the deer and the cattle being an aesthetic backdrop to the house as well as a source of food.

The seventeenth century saw formal design and rigid regularity imposed on existing and new parks.[13] Out went the semi-natural landscape of irregularly-shaped ancient woods, heath and grassland and in came straightness: straight tree-lined avenues and walks and straight canals, with vistas cut through existing woodlands to create views from the house over the park and the estate and in the opposite direction from the park to the house. Nature was put under strict human control.

There was a brief halt to development during the Commonwealth period after the execution of Charles I in 1649 until the reinstatement of the monarchy with the crowning of Charles II in 1660, when further development of existing parks and the creation of many new ones took place. Existing parks were enlarged, and tree planting became the rage, greatly influenced by the writings of John Evelyn.[14] The more trees, extending over more and more acres, were seen as a great status symbol, symbolising ownership and landed power. The word park came to be a synonym for house, park and estate and whole estates incorporated the name park in their name – local examples being Sandbeck Park and Kiveton Park.

Great swathes were cut through the planted trees, often in the shape of what the French called a *patte d'oie* (goose foot), a semi-circular space from which three, five or seven avenues radiated. And tree-lined avenues for riding and walking continued to be important – there were, for example, 4,000 planted trees in the avenues at Hampton Court by 1700. Avenues and canals were both features of the French royal park at Versailles created by le Notre and these began to be much imitated in England. In the last two decades of the century Dutch influence became increasingly significant, not only in the growing of tulips but in the introduction of topiary and

Stainborough Hall (later renamed Wentworth Castle) and its gardens as portrayed by Leendert Knyff and engraved by Jan Kip, c 1714.

The landscaped park at Wentworth Castle from across the serpentine lake with the Corinthian temple on the left, from an engraving, 1821.

water features, not only canals, but cascades and fountains.

Then in the eighteenth century came a great revolution in park design. Out went symmetry, orderliness and regularity and in came informality and naturalness. The eighteenth century was the great period of the landscaped park.[15]

There were a number of reasons for this great change. It has been said that it reflected political changes following the 'glorious revolution' of 1688 – the replacement of royal despotism by constitutional government – the freeing of the population from tyranny being accompanied, it has been strongly believed, by a desire to free the landscape from the clasp of rigid design. Another important influence that grew as the eighteenth century advanced was the strong impact that foreign travel had on the sons of the country's leading families during their Grand Tour on the continent of Europe. The landscapes they saw in Italy, with their classical ruins, and the landscape paintings they viewed, had a deep impact and there was an increasing desire to sweep away the regularity of the landscapes they were to inherit and to replace them with a more natural landscape. Another reason was supposed to be the great expense incurred in creating and maintaining heavily planted parks, although it must be said that in many cases their more natural successors proved to be just as expensive.

The new landscaped parks were characterised by hundreds of acres of rolling grassland, in some parks substantially re-contoured, by naturally shaped woodland and clumps of trees, and large expanses of water, usually created by widening and deepening the beds of streams to form winding lakes called serpentines. These natural-looking but often largely artificial landscapes were dotted with a range of buildings in a variety of architectural styles ranging from necessary edifices such as lodges at the entrances to the park, stable blocks, deersheds and boathouses, to the useful, such as temples and other roofed buildings with open sides from which the park could be viewed, and where tea and shelter from inclement weather could be taken during a circuit of the park on horseback or by carriage, to purely monumental obelisks, pyramids and mausoleums.

Many of these architectural features can still be seen in the landscaped parks in and around South Yorkshire. Wentworth Woodhouse has the greatest surviving collection of such features, many of them dating from the period 1723-50, during the time when Thomas Watson-Wentworth, 1st Marquis of Rockingham, was in residence. He meticulously recorded the changes that were taking place in the park at Wentworth. In 1729 he recorded that a keeper's lodge had been built, that the park perimeter had been walled and an obelisk erected in Lee Wood. He also recorded the building of what he called the 'Tempiatto' and an Ionic and a Doric temple, the latter two features surviving to this day. In 1729 he recorded that 'a piece of water of

The ha-ha at Cannon Hall with the garden on the left and the park on the right.

Ionic temple, Wentworth Woodhouse.

three Acres was made to flow from the Terrass between Shire Oaks & Old Hague [woods] and other lesser Waters for a Serpentine River'. Outside the park on one of the highest points on the estate, and clearly visible from inside the park, he built Hoober Stand. This 'Pyramidal Building', as he called it, was begun in 1747, in honour of King George II and the suppression of the 1745 Jacobite rebellion.[16]

The rolling grassland sometimes swept right up to the front door of newly-built mansions as it still does in South Yorkshire at Wentworth Woodhouse and Cusworth Hall and in West Yorkshire at Nostell Priory. In all three cases the garden was relegated to a position at the side of or behind the mansion. Where the garden fronted onto the park, existing walls were removed and were replaced by a ha-ha. This was a dry moat with a sloping side facing the park and with a vertical wall on the side nearest the

16

garden. The first recorded ha-ha in the country was constructed at Levens Hall in Cumbria in 1694 by Guillaume Beaumont. This sunken fence gave uninterrupted views from the house and garden across the landscaped parkland while at the same time ensuring that grazing deer, cattle or sheep did not trample or consume the garden plants. The derivation of the name *ha-ha* remains a mystery, although one possibility is that it is an onomatopoeic term reflecting either the expression of surprised delight uttered on viewing an exquisite park landscape from the garden and another is that it is an expression of the fear of falling into a ha-ha having come across it suddenly. Complete ha-has still survive separating the garden from the park at Cannon Hall and at Wortley Hall. Park perimeter ha-has separating the park from the farmed countryside beyond it have also survived on the edge of the parks at Nostell Priory and Bretton Hall and submerged on the park side of the serpentine lake at Cusworth Hall.

The eighteenth and first half of the nineteenth centuries also saw much park enlargement and re-alignment of boundaries, again often meticulously recorded by owners. Thomas Watson-Wentworth at Wentworth Woodhouse, for example, noted at the beginning of the 1740s that the total circumference of his park was 'six miles & seventeen Hundred & twenty two yards', but by 1744 he noted that it had been increased to more than nine miles.[17] The enlargement of Wentworth Park was largely the result of incorporating 261 acres of Greasbrough Common into the park as Thomas Wentworth's share in the Enclosure award of 1728 and buying a coppice wood, Scholes Coppice, in 1714 and which by 1726 was being 'cut into Walks for Beauty and intended to be thrown in the Park'.[18]

Great names are associated with the development of landscaped parks. Sir John Vanbrugh was associated at the beginning of the eighteenth century with the rebuilding of Castle Howard in North Yorkshire and the development of a contoured landscape with obelisks and temples in the classical style; Charles Bridgeman, who was closely associated (from 1713) with the development of Stowe in Buckinghamshire, which is widely regarded as the prototype of the landscaped park; William Kent, who was originally trained as a painter and whose motto was 'nature abhors a straight line' and who was associated with the development of parks containing clumps of trees, serpentine lakes and dotted with obelisks and temples evoking classical landscapes; Humphry Repton who has become best known for his 'Red Book' in which he portrayed a park as it was before he began his work and then what it would look like when he had finished; and of course, most famous of all, Lancelot 'Capability' Brown. It was Brown who struggled for eight years to re-design the park at Blenheim for the Duke of Marlbrough. He also worked in South Yorkshire, having been in charge of re-designing the park at Sandbeck Park and converting the remains of Roche Abbey into a romantic ruin ('with a poet's feeling and a painter's eye')[19] for the 4th Earl of Scarbrough between 1774 and 1777 at a cost of £3,000. In the park at Sandbeck he built a sunken fence (a ha-ha) created lakes, planted trees, laid out walks and a carriageway. Humphry Repton also did some late work on the park at Wentworth Woodhouse. A less well-known landscape designer who made the biggest impact in South Yorkshire was Richard Woods whose work at Cannon Hall and Cusworth Hall is described in detail in Chapter 4 of the book.

In the nineteenth century the plantings of the eighteenth century matured and the private landscaped parks of the previous century kept their essential outlines and character.[20] The last two centuries have, however, seen great changes of ownership and use of great country houses and their parks, nationally and locally. Some local houses and their parks and gardens like Nostell Priory, have come into the ownership of the National Trust, others, like Brodsworth, into the ownership of English Heritage, while others like Cannon Hall and Cusworth have been acquired by local authorities. Others like Bretton Hall, Wentworth Castle, Wentworth Woodhouse and Wortley Hall are in mixed ownership and/or occupation. Only one local house, garden and its park remains in family hands, Renishaw Hall.

One of the legacies of the landscaped park movement has been the way in which a number of its most characteristic features: the building of lodges at the main entrances, water features, planting of specimen trees, the placing of statues, obelisks and other architectural features about the park, and pavilions to provide resting places, shelter and places to take refreshment, were borrowed by the designers of urban public parks in the Victorian and Edwardian period.

Public parks

The parks discussed so far were private and predominantly rural. At the beginning of the nineteenth century only London had large urban parks: the royal parks – Hyde Park, Green Park, St James's Park, Kensington Gardens and Regent's Park – and these were gradually opened to the public, though entrance fees and selective opening hours were used to restrict entry on occasions. Almost all other urban parks – and they may not be called parks, they may be called botanical gardens or arboreta – are the legacy of the Victorian park movement, even those created after the end of the nineteenth century.[21]

The need for publicly-owned managed green spaces in Britain's towns and cities was gradually identified in the first three decades of the nineteenth century as the country rapidly urbanised and urban centres multiplied in number and spread outwards, leaving the urban population – there was no public transport to speak of – increasingly distant from country lanes and green footpaths and un-industrialised riversides. The rate of urbanisation and population growth was extremely high. In 1801 the population of England and Wales was 9.2 million. One hundred years later it was 32 million. Not only did the population grow rapidly, it was increasingly concentrated in urban areas. In 1801 only nineteen per cent of the population lived in areas with a population of over 20,000; by 1851 fifty-four per cent of the population was classified as urban and by 1911 the figure was eighty per cent. It must also be remembered that the urban populations, especially in the rapidly growing ports and industrial towns and cities, were overwhelmingly youthful and birth rates were high. There was no compulsory education until 1870 and adults and children alike among the working classes worked long hours. After work most returned to densely-packed housing areas where infectious diseases spread quickly. In these areas the only place that men could resort to when not working was the public house.

It was to these populations and to these types of area that the early park promoters turned their attention. They stressed the physical and social benefits of parks. Writing in a Sheffield newspaper as late as *c* 1900 a local journalist reporting about the number of boys he saw climbing the fences and walls to get into Hillsborough Park prompted him to note that:

An engraving of Sheffield Botanical Gardens showing subscribers promenading.

> *The joy of getting on to green sward and into fresh air must be great to many of them and half hours spent in a place like this must needs have a softening and civilising influence.*[22]

The motives of the early park promoters, however, were not entirely selfless and altruistic. It was argued that areas where the working classes could take supervised exercise in their spare time, and preferably in family groups, in a parkland atmosphere, would lead to a healthy workforce, promote stable families and dampen down unrest and militancy at work. They also believed that public parks would be places of social mixing thus easing the tensions between people of different classes. The governing classes were concerned at this time with the activities of the Chartist movement, a popular movement for electoral and social reform formed following the Reform Act of 1832 that left the mass of the population without a voice in the country's affairs. There were riots in Birmingham and throughout the north of England in 1839. The reaction of the local establishment is neatly summed up in the views of Alfred Gatty, a solicitor's son, educated at Eton (where his fag was the 6th Earl Fitzwilliam) and Oxford who came to be vicar of Ecclesfield in 1839:

The parish was rude and rough, notoriously so. Within living memory there were periodic bull and bear baitings, for which a bull and two bears were maintained. Dog and cockfighting were also popular sports ...

Nor was the surrounding neighbourhood into which we had come amiably affected. The whole district about Sheffield was violently disturbed by the spirit of Chartism. In January 1840, Sir Charles Napier, who had the military command, was informed by the colonel of dragoons at the barracks, that there was a conspiracy to burn and plunder the town; but the ringleader was cleverly captured by the chief constable and his assistant. Curiosity led me to the town hall when the leaders of the insurrection were examined; and their behaviour, with the implements of destruction that lay upon the table gave me an unpleasant sense of having found a home in a very riotous locality.[23]

Official recognition of the need for urban parks dates from 1833 when the Select Committee on Public Walks presented its report to Parliament. The report established that needs were greatest in Birmingham, Leeds, Liverpool and Manchester. London, of course, had its royal parks although provision in the East End of London was poor. The report did not distinguish between public open space and semi-public open space (eg, botanical gardens where only members could visit at any time, and the general public was only allowed in on certain occasions) so the situation was even worse than the Committee described.

In the decade following the publication of the Select Committee report numbers of pioneering parks were created. Preston has the distinction of being the first industrial town to create a municipal park, Moor Park, created by the enclosure of a common in 1833. In 1841 Derby Arboretum was created on land donated by the industrialist Joseph Strutt, and designed by John Claudius Loudon, one of the foremost landscape gardeners at that time. Rates could not be used by urban authorities at that time to maintain their parks so Derby Arboretum was maintained by subscribers and the general public were only allowed in on Wednesdays and on Sundays after the morning church services. Manchester acquired land for Philips Park and Queen's Park in 1845 after money had been raised by public subscription. Neighbouring Salford gained its first park – Peel Park – a year later. Birkenhead was the first of the local authorities to combine housing and park development in connection with Birkenhead Park in 1847. Joseph Paxton, the Duke of Devonshire's head gardener at Chatsworth, designed both Prince's Park in Liverpool and Birkenhead Park. South Yorkshire also saw the creation of two very early parks: Sheffield's Botanical Gardens (open on most days only to subscribing members) were opened in 1836 and in 1841 the Duke of Norfolk donated land for Norfolk Park in Sheffield – but this was for use of the land only and the Corporation did not acquire the site itself until 1909.

It was not until the *Towns Improvement Clauses Act* of 1847 that local authorities could buy or rent land specifically for recreation without a local Act of Parliament and they were still not allowed to maintain through the rates land that had been given to them for park development. The passing of the *10 Hour Act* (length of the working day) and the Saturday Half Holiday movement provided further stimuli for the municipal park movement and this was reinforced in 1859 by the *Recreation Grounds Act*, which encouraged the donation of money and land for park development, and the *1860 Public Improvements Act* which gave local authorities the

The Prince and Princess of Wales passing through a facsimile of Sheffield Castle, erected by the Duke of Norfolk, on their way to the opening of Firth Park. The Graphic, 21 August 1875

power to acquire and manage parks out of the rates. These acts inspired a further flurry of donations and park creations in the 1860s and 1870s. These included, in South Yorkshire, Locke Park in Barnsley in 1862, Firth Park and Weston Park in Sheffield both in 1875, and Rotherham Park (now Boston Castle Park) in 1876. What all these parks had in common was that they were reactive – they were developed to solve perceived problems long after, sometimes decades after, those problems had first arisen.

When the parks were opened, often by royalty, as in the case of Firth Park in Sheffield and Clifton Park in Rotherham in 1895, crowds were immense. And after they were opened they were very heavily used. On the day Victoria Park in London's East End opened in 1845, 25,000 people plunged into the bathing lakes before eight o'clock in the morning and on Whit Monday 1892 it was estimated that 305,000 strolled through the same park.

A number of park designers had an immense influence on features found in many relatively unknown parks. Loudon and Paxton have already been mentioned. Paxton's influence was particularly wide-ranging. F L Olmstead, the American park designer visited Paxton's Birkenhead Park twice in the mid-nineteenth century and later incorporated a number of Paxton's features into Central Park in New York City. Perhaps Paxton's most copied innovation was the raised terrace which he first used in the new Crystal Palace Gardens at Sydenham in south London, a more local example of which can be seen in his People's Park in Halifax. Paxton's ideas were also passed on to a number of younger park designers who trained with Paxton. Among other influential designers was William Barron who was trained at Edinburgh Botanical Gardens and became the head gardener at Elvaston Castle in Derbyshire before starting his own nursery and landscape design business in the 1850s. He often used some variation on a central or axial pathway threading its way through the designed landscape, as he did in Locke Park in Barnsley. Also of local significance was Robert Marnock, head gardener at Bretton Hall before he won the competition to design Sheffield Botanical Gardens. He became the curator there before leaving for London to design eighteen acres of and become curator of Regent's Park. He later designed Weston Park in Sheffield.

By the beginning of the last century the Victorian parks movement had transformed the face of Britain's towns and cities. But the amount, pattern and type of park provision varied enormously from one town and city to another. It would take the introduction of planning legislation (the *1909 Town Planning Act* which identified open spaces as a major planning concern and the 1947 *Town and Country Planning Act* with its emphasis on development plans which had to be approved by central government were both major steps forward) and the injection of new ideas on physical planning (particularly important was the neighbourhood principle introduced by the Garden City Movement which was the brainchild of Ebenezer Howard) before provision was rationalised. It is now estimated that there are 4,000 Victorian or Edwardian public parks in the United Kingdom together with 30,000 other public green spaces, altogether covering 140,000 hectares (350,000 acres).

Public parks played an important part in the lives of the British people during the Second World War. Not only were large amounts of parkland ploughed up for arable production, let as allotments or turned into grazing land for local farmers but they also became the venue for the 'Holidays at Home' schemes, essential local initiatives when travel for civilians was restricted and fear of an invasion put the coastal resorts

The bandstand, Locke Park.

out of bounds. Between 1941 and 1945, for example, the City of Sheffield Parks Department organised 1,806 events including military and brass band concerts, concert parties, light operatic shows, Punch and Judy shows, circuses, fun fairs, variety shows and open air dancing.

At the height of their popularity and place in civic pride – as late as the end of the 1960s in many cases – Britain's municipal parks were not only heavily used, they were also splendidly maintained and superintended. Their lodges were occupied by park keepers, they were surrounded (until the Second World War) by freshly painted cast iron railings and splendidly decorated iron gates, and inside there were immaculate carpet-bedding (and in many cases sculptured bedding) schemes, rock gardens, pruned shrubberies and bodies of water large and small. These meticulously kept grounds were punctuated by a range of un-vandalised and un-graffitied park buildings and other structures including refreshment shelters and pavilions in a variety of architectural styles, by bandstands, architectural ruins, bridges, drinking fountains and grottoes. From the beginning, too, there was provision for physical exercise, the giant stride being a great attraction in the 'gymnasium' area and often followed in due course by formal sporting areas such as football and cricket pitches, bowling greens, tennis courts and even skating rinks.

But things began to go downhill rapidly in the 1970s. The Bains Report of 1972 recommended the amalgamation of local authority Parks Departments with Leisure Services, and with local government re-organisation in 1974 Parks Departments lost their identity, and parks' managers had to vie for their budgets within the new Leisure Services departments that were often creating high-cost sports centres. Coupled with this, the provision of parks is not a statutory responsibility of local authorities and one way of cutting spending to avert rate-capping by central government was to reduce the costs (for maintenance, new equipment and salaries) of the parks for which they had responsibility.

At much the same time the Countryside Commission made available grants to local authorities to create and staff country parks in the urban fringe to prevent over-use by the car-owning public of the national parks and Areas of Outstanding Natural Beauty (AONBS). This again diverted attention and finance from the Victorian and later parks now embedded within the built-up areas of towns and cities.

Perhaps the most significant change was the introduction of Compulsory Competitive Tendering (now replaced by 'Best Value' contracting) brought in under the *Local Government Act* of 1988 when every maintenance job had to be put out to the lowest tender. The number of park staff was drastically reduced and the local

A giant stride. Bob Warburton

Forge Dam, Whiteley Woods, Sheffield.

authorities merely became the issuer of contracts to landscape businesses that had no connection with a particular park and its history, – 'roving gangs of grass cutters' as they have been described by traditionalists.

By the 1990s the nation's public parks were in deep crisis. The buildings in the parks were shabby or derelict, the grounds were often litter-strewn and dog-fouled, shrubs were overgrown, the once magnificent flower beds either gone or only a pale imitation of their former glory, the grassed areas brown or weed-infested. Lodges had been sold, seventy per cent of glasshouses had gone, fifty-six per cent of paddling pools had disappeared, as had many bandstands. They were not only under-resourced, but strategic greenspace planning was inadequate and there was a lack of local political commitment and leadership. Vandalism and neglect were everywhere in evidence.

Now things are changing for the better. There has been a realisation by local and central government that urban parks still have an important role to play in people's lives in the late twentieth and twenty-first centuries. They are psychological safety valves for people living highly pressured and stressful lives; they encourage healthy exercise; they are important social focal points for communities; they can enhance the image of a town or city and attract 'footloose' industries and other employers; and, finally, it has also been increasingly realised that historic urban parks deserve as much care as historic buildings.

Two significant forces in the changing fortunes of Britain's urban public parks are

Looking across the flower beds to the main gateway of Sheffield Botanical Gardens after refurbishment.

'people power' and the National Lottery. Now most historic parks have a 'Friends of...' group. Such groups badger, cajole and persuade their local authority to act positively and decisively and help to secure funding for park regeneration projects. The Heritage Lottery Fund launched its Urban Parks Initiative in 1998 to fund capital works and revenue costs (mainly fixed term staffing) in parks and in the last seven years has invested more than £380m in more than 240 parks across the country.[24] Some of the earliest schemes including Alexandra Park in Oldham, Sitwell Park in Gateshead and Battersea Park in London opened in a fully restored condition in the summer of 2004. Locally, the impact of the Heritage Lottery Fund can be seen in Sheffield in Norfolk Park and the Botanical Gardens.

$\mathscr{T}$HE ENGLISH ORNAMENTAL GARDEN

The Tudor and Stuart ornamental garden, *c* 1500-1700

The earliest English ornamental gardens for which we have a clear idea of layout and planting are from the Tudor period. As already noted in Chapter 1 the sixteenth century was a period of strong and stable central government which led to the abandonment of castles and fortified houses and the building of country houses (still sometimes surrounded by a moat). The period also saw the wealth of the country increase through the widening of foreign trade and the rise of new leading families and a substantial 'squirearchy'.

Both the leading aristocratic families and the country squires laid out formal ornamental gardens close to their houses, and, for those who could afford it, as discussed in Chapter 1, a park stretched beyond the garden. The ornamental garden was usually square or rectangular and surrounded by a hedge, trellis work or for the most affluent, a wall. This boundary fence was to keep out the wind and grazing animals from the surrounding park or neighbouring farmland.

The layout of the Tudor ornamental garden was formal and symmetrical. A common arrangement was for a central path to lead from the front of the house to a series of parterres which were level areas with ornamental gardens, laid out as knot

Open knots at Hodsock Priory with the late Elizabethan gatehouse in the background.

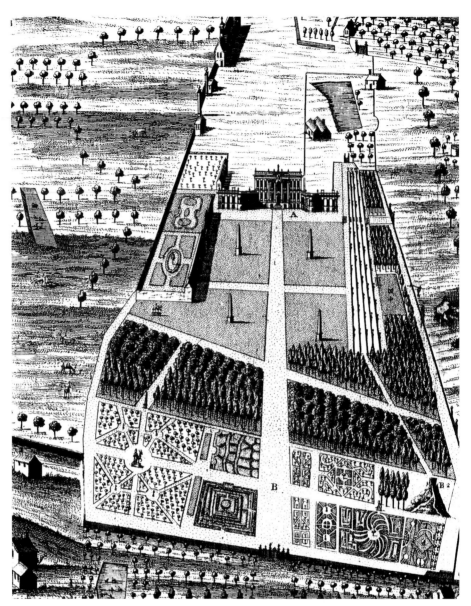

The gardens at Wentworth Woodhouse c 1730. Bodleian Library, Oxford

gardens. These usually square 'knotted beds' consisted of formal geometrical patterns formed by dwarf shrubs, most commonly box, or herbs, for example, thyme, hyssop, rosemary or thrift, which were kept closely clipped. The clippings were often collected and taken to the house to be strewn on the floor among the rushes to sweeten the smell of the indoor rooms. The spaces between the closely clipped shrubs or herbs were either planted with flowers such as primroses or daffodils or strewn with coloured earth, sand, pebbles, brick dust or broken pieces of terracotta. Flower-filled knots were known as 'closed knots'; those only filled with coloured earth and other non-plant colouring materials were called 'open knots'.[1] Some knots became mazes, sometimes cut low in box like the surrounding knots but sometimes in juniper, rising above shoulder height.

Between the house and the far end of the garden, below the enclosing walls or hedges, covered walks were constructed, of shrub-covered trellis work or clipped yew. The covered walks at Thornbury Castle in Gloucestershire, for example, were made of whitethorn and hazel with roses growing through the shrubs.[2] There would have been almost year-round colour or interest from the whitethorn blossom in spring, roses throughout the summer and hazel nuts and sloes in the autumn. The walks contained occasional arbours – sometimes in Tudor documents referred to as 'roosting places' – where members of the family or guests could rest, read or converse. Another important feature of the Tudor garden was the 'mount', an artificially made turfed hill which could be climbed via a winding path and from the top of which the knot gardens could be viewed as could the parkland beyond the ornamental garden boundaries. Often an arbour or a summer house was built on the summit of the mount. Strewn about the gardens of the highest in the land would be figures carved in timber and stone, but the more humble squire would be satisfied with a sundial or a fountain.

Another important feature of the ornamental garden in the second half of the sixteenth century was the raised terrace, which gradually replaced the mount. Most commonly this would run along the face of the house and a flight of steps would lead to a parterre made into a lawn or divided into knot gardens. There was sometimes another raised terrace at the far end of the garden with views over the surrounding park or back across the garden to the house. Small summer houses or garden houses were built at the end of the terraces.

As the years passed and the sixteenth century passed into the seventeenth, a greater variety of exotic flowers began to be grown in the gardens. For example, the Tradescants, father (died 1638) and son (died 1662), introduced from North America the tulip tree, the red maple, the lupin, phlox and aster (michaelmas daisy). Other North American introductions included goldenrod, evening primrose, French marigold and yucca.

Many features of the Tudor garden of the sixteenth century continued to be favoured throughout the seventeenth century and into the eighteenth century. One of the most celebrated accounts of an imaginary ornamental garden in the early seventeenth century came from the pen of Francis Bacon in 1625.[3] He said his mythical garden was to be in three parts: an entrance court or 'green', which was to be 'finely shorn', a main garden and a heath or wilderness. There were to be covered alleys in the garden where the visitor could walk 'in the great heat of the day'. In the middle of his garden he said he wished for a 'fair mount' thirty feet high with a summer house on top 'with some chimneys neatly cast and not much glass'. Bacon was not a fan of intricately patterned knots stating that if they were included in the garden they should be near the house so that they could be seen from the windows but he added contemptuously that 'you may see as good sights, many times, in tarts.'

Locally many features of a Tudor or Stuart garden survived at Wentworth Woodhouse into the second quarter of the eighteenth century and were portrayed in an engraving of *c* 1730. At that time the Palladian mansion that faces the park had not been built and the engraving shows the westward facing Baroque mansion with the walled ornamental garden laid out in front of it running to the main entrance in Hague Lane. In front of the house is a large lawn divided into four by a wide path and a central drive leading westwards to the gate on Hague Lane. In the centre of each quarter of the lawn stands a large obelisk which were recent additions to the garden. The 1st Marquis of Rockingham said they were in place by 1729, although he may later have regretted their prominent position when Horace Walpole said the view looked liked a bowling alley! On the south side of the lawn are five rows of what appear to be pleached trees, probably fruit trees, and beyond these near the south wall other planted trees and placed among them what is probably a bowling green. On the north side of the lawn are three walled beds. West of the lawn is another area of planted trees (a wilderness?) and beyond this a large area laid out mostly as knot gardens, one in a complicated whorl pattern and another looking like a maze. There are two statues on the walks between the beds. Several of the beds appear to contain shrubs and these may be roses. Lastly at the southern end of this area of the garden is a mount with winding paths climbing to its summit where there is a small tower.

The influence of Le Notre, the French garden designer, and his followers, was very important after the Restoration of King Charles II in 1660 when the straight avenues and canals of the French-influenced park also appeared at a smaller scale in the gardens of the period. And then in the last two decades of the seventeenth century the Dutch influence of topiary gardening came into its own, best exemplified in the magnificent topiary garden which still survives at Levens Hall in Cumbria and which dates from the 1690s.

The eighteenth century: studied simplification and informality
'Naturalness' was the keynote of garden design for most of the eighteenth century. Long straight lines in avenues of trees or canals or in geometrically planned walks through shrubs and trees gradually went out of fashion. In the early eighteenth century Joseph Addison wrote scathingly in *The Spectator* of the formal style of gardening found around every country house: 'We see the mark of the scissors on every plant or bush' he wrote, with every tree 'cut and trimmed into a mathematical figure'. He went on to say that in his opinion an orchard in flower was more

The topiary garden, Levens Hall, Cumbria.

Rhododendrons in the shrubbery at Wortley Hall.

delightful than 'all the labyrinths of the most finished parterre'. Topiary gardens that had at last grown to maturity were destroyed and straight avenues and formal groupings of trees were replaced by curving paths and informal 'wildernesses'. As the great Palladian mansions of the eighteenth century were finished, as has already been pointed out in Chapter 1, their landscaped parks often came up to the very walls of the house and the flower garden was relegated to the side or back of the mansion, sometimes in a screened walled enclosure. If a small flower garden survived, knotted beds disappeared and were replaced by much simpler circular or rectangular beds or by serpentine borders. Flowers were often relegated altogether to the kitchen garden.

A late eighteenth century landscaping style that embraced both garden and park was the 'Picturesque' style most closely associated with Sir Uvedale Price, a Herefordshire landowner. In his *Essays on the Picturesque* (1796) he criticised the monotony and blandness of William Kent's and Lancelot Brown's designs. Instead he was inspired by the Romantic artists such as Poussin and Claude and advocated a much more rustic and wild landscape style. Instead of Brown's smooth serpentine river banks, tonsured lawns and elegant groups of trees, Price favoured broken and crumbling river banks, rutted lanes and irregular groups of trees and shrubs. He put his ideas into practice on his own estate. Humphrey Repton, trained originally as a landscape painter, gradually adopted something akin to the Picturesque approach. Repton criticised Brown's 'mistaken system' of creating sweeping lawns up to the walls of the mansion, and often inserted a balustraded garden terrace between the house and the park.

Nineteenth and early twentieth century innovations

The nineteenth century saw a great many innovations that transformed existing gardens and resulted in the creation of completely new and exciting gardens. The new ideas, partly fuelled by the introduction from all parts of the globe of new flowering plants, shrubs and trees and hybridisation on a large scale, involved new planting schemes and the creation of specialised gardens. The work of a number of influential Victorian and Edwardian plant collectors (such as Robert Fortune, George Forrest and E H 'Chinese' Wilson), garden designers (such as Gertrude Jekyll) and writers (such as William Robinson and Reginald Farrer) also proved very influential.

Imposed naturalness in the garden, based on the planned disposition of trees and shrubs, which had been such an important feature of eighteenth century gardens continued to be of major significance in the nineteenth century. The 'Picturesque' style gave way to the 'Gardenesque' style, invented by John Loudon, in which the trees and shrubs, both native and exotic, were planted and managed in such places and in such a way that they would reach their peak of perfection of growth. These principles influenced the planting and design of Sheffield Botanical Gardens. Over time the eighteenth century wilderness became a shrubbery with rhododendrons, magnolias, and camellias, or a collector's garden or an arboretum with newly introduced trees such as the tulip tree, the ginkgo or the sequoia or even a single-species area such as a pinetum full of pines or a salicetum full of willows including the weeping willow from China. Much later in the century, in 1870, William Robinson introduced in his book of the same name, the idea of 'the wild garden' by 'naturalizing many beautiful plants of many regions of the earth in fields, woods, copses, (and) outer parts of pleasure grounds'.[4] In the twentieth century this idea has developed particularly into the woodland garden in which native or introduced shrubs, climbers and flowers are allowed to become naturalised in a native woodland environment. This is best seen locally at Hodsock Priory in north Nottinghamshire with native woodland carpeted with snowdrops in

Rhododendrons at Wortley Hall.

Azaleas at Wentworth Castle.

The fern dell at Brodsworth Hall.

Inset: *Drawing from a letter by Juliana Ewing, the Ecclesfield-born Victorian children's writer, to her husband, showing her collecting ferns.*

February and March and at Renishaw Hall where the Wilderness is carpeted with bluebells in May and where a new woodland garden has recently been opened to the public.

Part of a shrubbery in the nineteenth century might well be converted into a fernery, although the early taste was to plant the ferns among rocks. Search parties from botanical societies would scour the countryside for abnormal forms for planting in their ferneries or growing in glass-covered cases in the drawing room. Nurserymen would offer for sale an astounding number of varieties of native hardy ferns, with as many as twenty varieties of the common male fern and lady fern and more than fifty varieties of hart's tongue fern being listed in a catalogue in the 1850s.[5] The only garden fernery still in existence locally is in the recently re-planted 'fern dell' at Brodsworth Hall. Just as popular as growing hardy ferns was the cultivation of exotic ferns in greenhouses. One of the fourteen subsidiary houses running off the palm

34

house in the new glasshouse complex at Wentworth Woodhouse in 1908 was a forty-foot long fernery.

In the previous century flowers had been of minor importance in gardens but in the nineteenth century they became of prime importance. The nineteenth century saw the introduction of the bedding system and the rise to the greatest importance of the herbaceous border.

The bedding system became a popular way of filling with colour the fashionable Italian style of garden with its terraces, balustrades, flights of steps with judiciously positioned statues and urns. The 'bedding craze' began about 1850 with the introduction from abroad of brightly coloured annuals such as calceolaria, scarlet geranium and verbena which had to be sown and raised under glass and planted out in the early summer after the last frosts had disappeared. Variations on the bedding system included ribbon borders in which bedding plants were grown in wide uninterrupted lines, sometimes for hundreds of yards beside a

Hollihocks.

drive or pathway; carpet bedding in which succulents replaced flowering plants in very tightly planted masses in intricate patterns like an oriental carpet or a clock in which the hands kept the right time; and three-dimensional or sculptural bedding in which bedding plants were grown around frames to look like, for example, a staircase or a regal crown. With the decline of flower bedding in public parks this type of bedding has now become very popular in such places as the entrance to a town hall or in the centre of an important road roundabout.

Residents and visitors will have admired the sculptured bedding figure of the crucible teemer outside Sheffield Town Hall in 2004 and motorists travelling through Doncaster will have gazed with wonder at the jet aeroplane, the Mallard train and a three-piece suite on islands at roundabouts in the town.

The bedding system eventually declined in general popularity. It was expensive, consumed a great deal of gardening staff time, and was thought by many to be vulgar and gaudy. Moreover if spring bedding was superseded by summer bedding, the spring bedding was removed while still in flower, and, if only summer bedding was used, the garden was bare throughout the spring. William Robinson in *The English Flower Garden* (1883) recalled walking through his local woods at the end of March when they were carpeted with primroses and wood anemones and then passing the villagers' gardens which were sprinkled with the flowers of a variety of native annuals and daffodils, aubretia and arabis. He then came to the 'villa gardens' awaiting their bedding plants, 'a blank, and showed no more signs of spring than they did at Christmas'.[6]

Although the bedding system continued to be, and still continues to be, a

Spring bedding at Brodsworth Hall.

feature of some private gardens (for example spring and summer bedding schemes are important features of the Italianate Brodsworth Hall garden) and some public parks, it has attracted vehement criticism from various critics who were concerned about the neglect of herbaceous perennials. The most famous critic of carpet bedding was William Robinson, already quoted above. So incensed was Robinson by the concentration on the bedding system in the Irish garden where he was in charge of the greenhouses that in 1861 in a great rage he is said to have extinguished all the heat in the greenhouses where the bedding plants were being raised, opened all the windows to the cold winter air and left his employment. Another prominent critic was Shirley Hibberd, who in his *Amateur's Flower Garden* published in 1871, wrote disparagingly of 'the most gorgeous display of bedding plants … like the blazing fire at the mouth of the coal-pit.' Hibberd said that the four essentials of a garden were a few trees and shrubs, a plot of grass, comfortable walks and the hardy herbaceous border. This is thought to be one of the very earliest pieces of modern advocacy for what had been the old fashioned mixed border. In the same year William Sutherland, retired former head of the Herbaceous Department at Kew Gardens, brought out a book devoted largely to herbaceous plants and he advocated the planting of mixed borders.[7] The spread of herbaceous or mixed borders, either as island beds or against a sunny wall, saw the rise in popularity of an astonishing variety of perennials, both native and introduced, which found their true home there: the delphinium, erigeron, foxglove, hollyhock, hosta, lupin, penstemon, peony, phlox, poppy, and red hot poker to name just a few of the most reliable and colourful.

Towards the end of the century the move away from bedding to herbaceous planting was greatly aided by the influence of Gertrude Jekyll (1843-1932), writer (more than 1,000 gardening articles and sixteen gardening books) and garden designer (with about 350 garden design commissions) who published plans for herbaceous borders for early, middle and late flowering, created wonderful gradations of colour in borders and special colour gardens.[8] Her gardens were marked by restraint, regard for the rules of colour harmony with the occasional colour surprise. In her own garden at Munstead Wood in Surrey she created a series of compartments that could be viewed separately, an idea that has been much imitated in the twentieth century, most supremely at Hidcote Manor in Gloucestershire, now the property of the National Trust.

It was also during the nineteenth century that the rock garden became the alpine garden. The first alpine garden, rather than a rock garden, which is known to have existed for at least two centuries, was created in 1859 by the nursery firm of Backhouse of York. In 1865 the firm published the first catalogue devoted entirely to alpine plants and the popularity of alpines and of creating an alpine garden increased as the development of the continental railway network made holidays in Switzerland a must for the middle and upper classes. In the early twentieth century the writings of Reginald Farrer (who gardened on the slopes of Ingleborough and who invented the scree garden) and Clarence Elliott (who was involved in the design and planting of Whinfell Quarry Gardens in Sheffield) encouraged the creation of more large alpine gardens.

'Pastiche' gardens, mimicking gardens of different times and different places and cultures were also a feature of the nineteenth and early twentieth centuries. The Italianate gardens have already been noted. Another, the Japanese garden, with its pool, bridge, lanterns and perhaps a tea house and featuring Japanese shrubs such as

Japanese Garden at Tatton Park, Cheshire.

Horse-drawn lawnmower, Clifton Park.

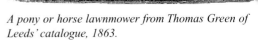

wisteria and Acer palmatum, cropped up in the most unusual places in the late nineteenth and early twentieth centuries inspired by a number of Japanese exhibitions in London and by Joseph Conder's *Landscape Gardening in Japan* (1903).[9] Such was the western interpretation of the real Japanese garden, that when shown round one at Friar Park in Oxfordshire, the Japanese ambassador is said to have commented: 'Magnificent. We have

A pony or horse lawnmower from Thomas Green of Leeds' catalogue, 1863.

nothing like it in Japan'. The nearest complete Japanese garden to South Yorkshire, restored in 2001, is at Tatton Park in Cheshire and the only local garden with Japanese features is at Wentworth Woodhouse.

Finally, no account of changes in the garden in the nineteenth century would be complete without reference to the lawn mower which replaced the back-breaking task of cutting grass with a scythe. Invented in 1830 by Edwin Budding and improved and increased in size and power in the 1840s and 1850s, the horse-drawn and, in the twentieth century, the motorised mower ensured the rising popularity of the closely mown lawn as the proper setting against which to view shrubberies, wild gardens, herbaceous borders and in which to cut out geometrical beds for bulbs and annuals.

$\mathcal{T}$HE COUNTRY HOUSE KITCHEN GARDEN

3

I n the early twenty-first century we can go down to our local superstore at any time of the year and pick from the shelves an enormous variety of fresh vegetables, fruit and cut flowers flown in from every part of the world: for example, onions from New Zealand, beans from Morocco, tomatoes from Spain, conference pears from Holland, nectarines from Italy and bananas from the Ivory Coast. But until comparatively recently this was not the case. Most people had to wait until that part of the year when domestic supplies were ready for picking or for digging up and ordinary people rarely saw fresh exotic fruit: an orange for Christmas was a great treat to be found in the stocking and pawpaws, avocadoes and lychees were unheard of.

People were very much dependent upon what grew in their own or in their neighbours' gardens: at one end of the social scale in the cottage garden attached to a cottage of a worker in the countryside or in the allotment of an industrial worker or town dweller, and at the other end of the social scale in the kitchen garden attached to the large house of a wealthy industrialist, professional man, country squire or grand aristocrat.

Allotments and domestic vegetable gardens still survive but more as a hobby rather than a necessity while the many country house gardens, the subject of this chapter,[1] have largely ceased their original function unless part of a visitor attraction. But survive they do and they provide enormous pleasure, as well as being an important instructive and educational resource.

Size, layout and location of the country house kitchen garden

Most country house kitchen gardens were centred upon a rectangular-shaped walled garden ranging in size from one acre in the case of a professional family to twenty or thirty acres if it belonged to one of the leading aristocratic families who had not only their immediate families to feed but also a continuous flow of guests and armies of indoor and outdoor servants and estate workers. It was

The entrance gate to the kitchen garden at Wortley Hall.

Glasshouse in the kitchen garden at Cannon Hall.

reckoned that an acre of walled kitchen garden would feed about a dozen people throughout the year.[2] The walled kitchen garden at Cannon Hall is three acres in extent, that at Wentworth Woodhouse was four acres and the one at Wortley Hall five acres. The Duke of Portland's kitchen garden at Welbeck Abbey in Nottinghamshire (now the Dukeries Garden Centre), covered twenty acres.

The walls, often as high as twelve feet, were usually of brick, which was a good storer and transmitter of the sun's heat. The walls had a number of important functions. The shelter they provided resulted in an improved microclimate within the walls and also immediately to the south of the southern wall or to the east of the eastern wall, where an extra sheltered garden, called a slip garden, was often laid out making use of the wall for growing fruit and the ground in front for vegetables and flowers. A large slip garden existed outside the southern wall of the kitchen garden at Wentworth Woodhouse and beyond the eastern wall at Cannon Hall. The roughly east-west, north-south alignment of a walled garden (they were often built at an angle with the northern and southern walls running NNW-SSE or SSW-NNE) also meant that fruit and vegetables would be ready over a longer period of time than those grown in an open garden, with those growing on the north face of the south wall ripening later than those on the south-facing north wall and those on the west-facing east wall. Exotic fruits such as peaches and nectarines and vines were often grown under the protection of glass or netting, mats and canvas on the south-facing wall.

The entrances into the walled garden varied in their size and importance. For the gardeners there were usually small doorways, from the direction of the worksheds or the neighbouring frame yard. But for the owner, his family and his guests there was often an imposing gateway. At Wortley Hall, for example, there is a large gateway into the kitchen garden from the direction of the holly hedge avenue that leads from the ornamental garden. At Wentworth Woodhouse there was a central drive through the pleasure grounds from the main doorway of the west front of the mansion which eventually went through the centre of the kitchen garden via a large gateway with, on the top of the gate posts, statues of Lucretia and Collatinus. At Clumber from the early years of the twentieth century, a wide driveway northwards from the house, passed through large gateways through the kitchen garden and finished at the entrance to the conservatory and palm house.

The ground inside the walled kitchen garden was meticulously planned and laid out. There were usually borders, normally at least as wide as the height of the walls, extending inwards from each of the four walls and ending in a wide gravel or cinder path that ran round the entire garden. The large internal rectangle of the garden was often then divided into a number of sections, called quarters, even though there could be only two or perhaps six or eight. Each section was bordered by a wide gravel or cinder path. The gravel or cinder paths in kitchen gardens were kept meticulously clean – gardeners were expected to use the boot scrapers that were located at the edges of the planted areas around the garden. Even the horses that pulled carts heaped with manure around walled kitchen gardens wore special leather shoes to prevent them churning up the paths. The paths were periodically raked by garden boys, especially if a visit from the owner or a member of his family was expected. Geoffrey Steer, who worked as a boy gardener at Wentworth Woodhouse before the Second World War, remembers that an important job on Saturday morning was raking the paths from the western door of the mansion through the Pleasure Grounds and the kitchen garden (a distance of about a mile) and polishing the brass door knobs and locks on all the glasshouses, full time jobs all morning for two boys.[3] The reason for this careful work was that in fine weather, on Sunday mornings, Earl and Countess Fitzwilliam and their family and guests would walk from the mansion along the garden path to the church service, and on the way back they would inspect the kitchen garden and glasshouses. Geoff remembers that if he left any brasso on a knob, Mr Third, the head gardener, would give him a whack with his felt hat.

To prevent soil spreading from the cultivated sections of the garden on to the paths, the cultivated ground was edged in different ways, sometimes by low box hedging, by tiles, and by low-growing flowers or culinary herbs such as London Pride, strawberries, thyme or parsley, often backed by cordon and espalier fruits.

Inside or outside the walls, depending on the size of the walled garden, were usually a series of glasshouses, frames, compost heaps, possibly an orchard, and built against the outside of the northern wall of the kitchen garden or against a series of glasshouses were the boiler house and a series of worksheds. A pond to supply water for the garden was built in some cases in the centre of the garden but where large amounts of water were required this would have been outside the walled garden. Here would also be a head gardener's house and a bothy for the accommodation of unmarried under gardeners. Beyond the north wall well away from the glasshouses and frames a shelter belt of trees may also have been planted.

Some kitchen gardens are quite near the mansion, others are some distance away well out of sight (and smell!). An important factor in locating a kitchen garden was the easy availability of manure, so there is often a close association between the site of the kitchen garden and the location of the stable yard and the home farm. At Wortley Hall the kitchen garden is immediately behind the stable block, and at Wentworth Woodhouse and Nostell Priory it was very near both the Home Farm and the stables.

Production in and maintenance of the country house kitchen garden
As has already been pointed out, the kitchen garden at a country house was the source of all vegetables, herbs, fruit, pot plants and cut flowers every day of the year. This was achieved in a number of different ways. Some vegetables were forced out of season in frames, hotbeds and closed sheds. Vegetables and fruits were also delayed in maturing or fruiting by growing them in a sheltered spot below a north wall. And fruits were grown against the walls, and depending on which wall they were grown, and whether glass was used, fruiting could be accelerated or delayed. In the north of England acceleration of fruiting and protection against late frosts was not only aided by draping the wall fruits in canvas and matting or erecting portable glass shelters against the walls but also through the expedient of making the walls themselves into 'hot walls'. Hot walls had internal flues fuelled by furnaces with the hot air escaping through chimneys on the tops of the walls. The north and south walls of the kitchen garden at Wentworth Woodhouse were hot walls and the outlines of nine fire houses that supplied the heat can still be seen on the north side of the north wall. The kitchen garden walls at Hillsborough House, now the Garden of Remembrance for the Hillsborough football disaster, were also hot walls and the evidence is again still visible.

Espaliered pear tree in the kitchen garden at Cannon Hall. Inset: Kitchen garden wall covered with old nails.

An enormous amount of time and effort was spent in pruning and supporting the fanned trees (usually peaches, nectarines, apricots and morello cherries) or espaliered (pears, apples, plums and cherries) fruit trees. Nails were bought in their thousands and close inspection of the walls of a country house kitchen garden will still reveal hundreds of rusty nails protruding from the mortar between the lines of bricks and thousands of nail holes. In the eighteenth century and earlier the fruit trees were attached to the nails with cuttings of cloth called 'shreads' or 'lists' obtained from woollen manufacturers or tailors, but the woollen shreds had been replaced by tarred twine by the nineteenth century.

Great efforts were made to rid the kitchen garden and its associated glasshouses of pests and diseases, proprietary insecticides and weed killers not being available until towards the end of the nineteenth century. Soft soap, sulphur, tobacco, paraffin, lime and gunpowder were all used widely against insect pests. Soft soap was lathered into fruit trees to rid them of aphids and plant lice and a strong soapy water was used against thrips.

Sulphur was sprinkled under plants to rid them of ants or fumigated to get rid of red spiders; tobacco water was syringed or brushed or fumigated onto plant leaves to get rid of aphids; diluted paraffin was washed onto plants to remove mealy bugs; lime was sprinkled over caterpillars, slugs and snails; and gunpowder was used to make 'squibs' to remove wasps' nests. In the glasshouses bottles were hung up filled with honeyed water to kill flies by drowning. Animals were also deterred from visiting the garden by setting mouse traps, sparrow traps and putting down rat poison. In many kitchen gardens a cat was employed to patrol the beds!

Orders were placed with seedsmen and nurserymen far and wide to supply the seeds and plants for the kitchen garden, G & J Telford of York and J & G Perfect of Pontefract cropping up most commonly in the accounts of a number of local kitchen gardens in the eighteenth century, and from Perfects and Backhouse of York (who had succeeded the Telfords) in the nineteenth century. And the variety of vegetables ordered was enormous. For example, the orders to Telfords and Perfects in 1790 from the head gardener at Wentworth Woodhouse consisted of seven varieties of beans, six varieties of peas, six varieties of lettuce, four varieties of cabbage, three of broccoli and two varieties each of onion, turnip and radish. The orders also included celery, parsley, spinach, red beet, endive, asparagus and a selection of culinary herbs. Also included were now hardly heard of vegetables such as orache (used as an alternative to spinach), cardoon (a thistle like vegetable related to globe artichoke), salsify (a root vegetable that apparently tastes like oysters) and scorzonera (a parsnip-like root vegetable).[4]

Great attention was also paid to increasing the variety of fruits grown up the kitchen garden walls and under glass. For example, an order for Cannon Hall in 1761 included a long list of fruit trees: fourteen varieties of peaches, six of nectarines, six of apricots, six of cherries, sixteen of plums and five of pears.[5] Another order in 1785 to J & G Perfect's nursery, this time from the head gardener at Cusworth Hall included, among a wide variety of trees, shrubs and herbaceous plants requests for twenty apple trees, standards and dwarfs of various varieties, eight pear trees, four cherry trees, two cornelian cherry trees and one 'barberry without stone'.[6]

Under glass in the eighteenth century were grown peaches, nectarines, apricots, oranges, and grapes for the table. Oranges were, of course, grown in the orangery, vines in the vinery and pineapples in the pinery. An orangery in a bad state

Top to bottom: apple saw fly, strawberry mite, fruit thrip, leaf hopper. Joseph Bentley Ltd, Barrow-on-Humber, Lincs, catalogue, p 117, 1939-40

*A pineapple
growing in a tan
pit in a pinery.*

of repair still survives in the kitchen garden at Wentworth Castle, and in the vinery at Cannon Hall, still fruiting copiously, is the two hundred year-old Muscat grape. But perhaps it was the pineapple that stirred owners most to compete with their neighbours, at first in growing them and getting them to fruit at all, and then in the number produced each year, then at the earliest date at which the ripe fruit was ready and finally in the size of the fruit.

It is believed that the first pineapple was grown in England in the late 1670s when gardener John Rose presented one to King Charles II. But pineapple growing on any scale did not begin until the 1720s and by the 1730s large landowners were said to be in the grip of 'Pineapple Fever'. The pineapples were first grown in so-called 'tan-pits'. Tan pits were brick-lined pits sometimes with a back wall to which sloping glass frames were fixed. The brick pits were then filled with a layer of rubble on which used tan bark was laid that would remain in place for between three and six months. Tan bark, which had first been used for horticultural purposes in Holland, was waste oak bark from leather tanning yards. While used oak bark was fermenting it produced a constant temperature to the roots of between 75-85 degrees Fahrenheit. The pineapples were grown in pots sunk into the tan bark from March to October. In October they were moved into heated glasshouses or 'stoves' and then moved back into the tan pits in spring. Eventually all-year-round pineries were built incorporating bark pits and heating from warm-air flues and later hot

water boilers. Checking on the heat of the soil in the tan pits led to the invention of the garden thermometer.

Glasshouse production of fruit, flowers and vegetables took a great step forward in the 1820s and 1830s with the development of coal-fuelled boilers which pumped hot water in pipes around the various glasshouses, the development of plate glass and the replacement of wooden structures by cast and wrought iron. It was in the subsequent hundred years that new complexes of glasshouses were erected on many country house estates. Unfortunately the large range of glasshouses built at Wentworth Woodhouse in 1908 by Mackenzie & Moncur of Edinburgh was demolished in the 1950s and 1960s. The main building consisted of a massive plant house with a central palm and plant corridor 200 feet long and twenty feet wide with fourteen subsidiary plant houses leading off the central corridor.[7] The most complete local glasshouse complex still standing and in full use is at Clumber Park. This 450 feet long, largely lean-to, complex is arranged south-facing along the north wall of the kitchen garden and also dates from 1908. It incorporates vineries, peach houses, a span-shaped palm house and a conservatory.

It was also the head gardener's responsibility to collect and store ice from ponds and lakes in the grounds. In the days before refrigeration this ice was used for storing meat and fish in the summer months and for making desserts and cooling wines. The ice was stored in a special structure called an ice-house.[8] In many cases the ice-house was located in the park at a not too inconvenient distance from the mansion, but in some cases it was located much nearer the big house concealed in some part of the gardens. It usually consisted of an entrance chamber leading to an often domed storage chamber which was sunk below ground level. The roof was sometimes thatched. Ice-houses still survive in a dilapidated state at Wortley Hall, Cannon Hall and Nostell Priory.

Apples: Gascoyne's Scarlet, Charles Ross and Allington Pippin. Robert Thompson, The Gardener's Assistant, Vol 4, 1901

Ice-house, Holkham Park, Norfolk.

The workforce, workers' housing and the worksheds

Garden workforces in the eighteenth and nineteenth centuries at the height of country house living were of a large size. In 1790, for example, the head gardener at Wentworth Woodhouse had under him twenty-seven gardeners. All but three of these were 'common labourers' including four females who no doubt did the most menial of tasks such as weeding.[9] The other three were two foremen and a carter. By the mid-nineteenth century the labour force was between forty and fifty with the annual wages bill over £1,000. In 1905 at Clumber House, the head gardener employed twenty-nine gardeners with an annual wages bill of about £1,000. A hierarchical system of employment emerged in which a boy might be taken on as an apprentice in his early teens, then become an improver journeyman, and then a

A group of gardeners with their domestic servant at Cannon Hall. Courtesy of Cannon Hall Museum

The head gardener's house, Clumber Park.

journeyman proper and eventually a departmental foreman (e.g., in the vegetable garden (outdoor) or the glasshouses (indoor). After a number of years as foreman he would be in a position to apply for the post of head gardener.

The head gardener reigned supreme in the gardens of a large country house; he was as important as the highest-ranking indoor servant. When appointed it was expected that the head gardener would stay for a considerable period of time and he certainly did in a number of known local cases. For example, at Wentworth Woodhouse, Benjamin Henderson was already in post when the new kitchen garden was being created in 1786 and he was there for almost another thirty years, dying in post in 1815. He was succeeded by George Thompson who was in post for another thirty years, being succeeded by Joseph Henderson in 1845. Henderson held the position for nearly twenty years. Another long-term incumbent was Samuel Barker who was head gardener at Clumber from 1899 to 1935.

Garden staff were recruited from far and wide even before the development of public transport systems. Many head gardeners in English country house gardens were Scottish. The head gardener was usually accommodated in a head gardener's house very near to the kitchen garden where a close eye could be kept on the glasshouses. At Castle Howard in North Yorkshire the head gardener's house was actually in the middle of the large kitchen garden. In some cases it was built into the kitchen garden wall but more often than not it was located just outside the walled garden, most often on the north side behind or beside the worksheds. Head gardeners' houses can be seen locally at Clumber just outside the walled garden, at Wortley Hall beside the worksheds (now called Avenue Cottage) and at Cannon Hall, squeezed between the mansion and the walled garden. Married garden labourers and foremen lived with their families in estate cottages and the garden boys also lived with their families in the local village. But unmarried men from outside the immediate locality were accommodated in a bothy just outside the kitchen garden walls. This had the double advantage of making sure young staff got to work on time and of always having young workers on hand to do extra watering, feed the boilers or adjust the ventilation in the glasshouses on Sundays.

The length of the working day was usually governed by the work bell which might be located at the entrance to the kitchen garden or at the neighbouring stables or home farm. Its loud clanging sound would be within hearing distance of all the outdoor estate workers. The workforce got up very early for most of the year. A set of 'orders and regulations' have survived for the gardens at Wentworth Woodhouse for 1863 which show that from the beginning of April until the end of September work started at six o'clock in the morning and finished at six o'clock at night; in March and October work began at 6.30 am and finished at 5.30 pm; in February and November the hours of work were from 7 am to 5 pm and in January and December from 7.45 am to 4.30 pm. Work took place six days a week finishing at 4 pm on Saturdays. The bell was also rung at noon for an hour's dinner break. Once a fortnight on Fridays the lunch break lasted till 1.30 pm so that wages could be paid when workers would have waited in line at the head gardener's office.[10]

Garden bell at Ripley Castle gardens, North Yorkshire.

The head gardener's office was usually one of the rooms in the line of worksheds, called the back sheds, built along the outside of the kitchen garden north wall or

Gardeners' mess room in the worksheds at Clumber Park kitchen garden.

along the outside of a vinery or other hothouse range either inside or outside the walled garden. At Clumber, for example, the worksheds are built on the outside of the north wall (now a museum of kitchen garden history), as they are at Wortley Hall (now incongruously converted into two private houses). At Cannon Hall worksheds can be seen within the walled garden behind the most northerly range of glasshouses, and at Wentworth Woodhouse they still survive behind the high brick wall of the vinery (the glass part of the structure having now been demolished) built in 1908.

Besides the head gardener's office, there was a series of worksheds and storage sheds and most importantly the boiler room which was in a cellar surrounded by coal bunkers, the building above being topped by a tall chimney one of which is still well in evidence at Wortley Hall and another at Clumber Park. The other rooms included a potting shed where seeds were sown and seedlings pricked out and re-potted, and where plant pots were scrubbed and cleaned. There were also cool storage sheds for apples, pears and other hard fruits, a grape store where branches carrying bunches of grapes were stored in specially made storage bottles, and possibly a mushroom house and a rhubarb shed. The range of sheds also contained the gardeners' mess room, warmed by its own fire, where the gardeners had their lunch break. It was the most junior garden boy's task to light the fire there not only to provide much needed warmth on cold days but also to heat the gardeners' tea bottles.

$\mathcal{V}$ISITOR GUIDE

BARNSLEY'S URBAN PUBLIC PARKS

Opened in 1862, Locke Park is Barnsley's only Victorian urban park. Although not selected for individual discussion here, Elsecar Park also has historic pretensions, the reservoir-side location of the site attracting to it the title of 'Elsecar by the Sea' at the beginning of the twentieth century. Elsecar Park also has the distinction of having a surviving early bandstand.

LOCKE PARK

Location: About one mile south-west from the centre of Barnsley. Accessed on foot either from Park Road (A6133), Racecommon Lane or by car from Keresforth Hall Road where there is a car park.
Facilities: About 46 acres of parkland with historic lodges. Small children's play area and two bowling greens.
Special features: Observation tower, bandstand, bronze statue of Joseph Locke (all Grade II listed) and four Ionic columns.

'Associated with the triumphs of the locomotive ...'

Locke Park, part of which opened in 1862, owes its origins to the Locke family. Joseph Locke (1805-1860) came to Barnsley as a five year old from Attercliffe. He was educated at the Holgate Grammar School before being apprenticed at Pelaw Colliery in County Durham where he began a lifelong friendship with Robert Stephenson.[1] Joseph Locke, together with Robert Stephenson and Isambard Kingdom Brunel, became the foremost specialists and leading authorities on all aspects of railway engineering. Joseph Locke is said to have engineered more miles of railway line than anyone in Britain and founded the continental rail system. When Locke returned to Barnsley on visits in the 1850s he enjoyed 'celebrity status' and he became one of Barnsley's most noted benefactors.[2] He died suddenly when on holiday in 1860.

After his death his widow, Phoebe, in accordance with her husband's wishes, purchased seventeen acres of land in Barnsley, known as High Style Field, and provided money for laying out the grounds as a new public park. It was then presented to the Town in

Joseph Locke's statue by Baron Marochetti.

51

memory of her husband. The park was opened amid great pomp and ceremony on 10 June 1862 and to mark the opening a commemorative medallion was cast. John Hugh Burland, a local historian and poet, composed a poem in Joseph Locke's honour. It described Locke's engineering skills and expertise – a man

> *Who bridged the sweeping flood,*
> *Who bored the Alpine chain,*
> *Who filled the chasms deep.*
> *Mid precipices steep,*
> *For the girded iron way.*

Burland also extolled the splendour of the new park where Barnsley folk could 'hear the lark', enjoy the 'shrubs and tree' and be forever free.[3]

The Institute of Civil Engineers commissioned a large bronze statue of Joseph Locke from the Italian sculptor, Baron Marochetti. It was intended for St Margaret's Garden in Westminster, London, beside those of Stephenson and Brunel but permission was denied. It was, therefore, placed in Locke Park in January 1866 to 'salutes and rifle fire.'[4] In 1879 stone balustrades were placed round the statue.

To quench the thirst

In October 1866 a stone fountain was erected in Locke Park with a metal cup and chain – a welcome sight on a hot summer's day. It started its life in Peel Square, Barnsley, having been purchased by subscription under the auspices of the Sunday School Band of Hope Union.[5] The aim of providing a drinking fountain was, apparently, to deter the thirsty from visiting a public house!

Stone drinking fountain in Locke Park. Chris Sharp, 'Old Barnsley'

Further gifts and developments

On 7 August 1877 Sarah McCreery, Phoebe's sister, formally presented a further twenty-one acres of land to Locke Park having erected a new lodge and 'railed the whole'. She had a splendid observation tower built in memory of her sister who had died in 1866. The tower was designed by R Renee Spiers and built by a local firm, Robinson and Son. It is now in need of renovation. Again, a commemorative medallion was issued in honour of Miss McCreery's gift. 'Memorial odes, moral songs and musings' were composed to the Lockes, Miss McCreery and F W T Vernon-Wentworth (who had given a small adjoining plot near Keresforth Hall Road).

The formal gardens (known as the Quarry or Valley Gardens) were designed by William Barron and Son of Elvaston Nurseries near Derby with a simple axial winding path forming the spine of the plan.[5] In 1879 a fountain was erected here as a 'tribute of gratitude to Miss McCreery by the Working Men of Barnsley.'[6] This formed a focal point along the main pathway of the gardens. Unfortunately water no longer cascades from this structure. Old postcards show amazing 'ribbon planting' on either side of this walkway. The colourful plants were graded in height with one species for each band of the ribbon – a tradition that continued for decades. At the southern end of this area are four Ionic columns once part of a building in the town known as the Commerce Building. When this building was redesigned in 1879 Barnsley Council bought the columns and placed them in Locke Park.

Observation Tower.

Enjoying music

After years of deliberation Barnsley Council eventually commissioned a bandstand for Locke Park from the Lion Foundry Co Ltd in Kirkintilloch at a cost of £326. When it was opened in June 1908 a crowd of 25,000 people was treated to a rousing

Ribbon planting in the Quarry or Valley Gardens.

Locke Park Quarry, Barnsley

performance from the Barnsley Volunteers' Band. The Friends of Locke Park have recently repaired and repainted this attractive structure and concerts are once again being held here. The original ornamental iron balustrade and some decorative ironwork have been lost as has the copper roof. Bandstands from this period are increasingly rare and this is a treasure that needs to be preserved.

Plans for the Future
A feasibility study for improvements to and the regeneration of Locke Park has been produced by Land Use Consultants for Barnsley Council. If funding can be secured it is intended that a new visitor centre with a restaurant and multi-purpose indoor sport and play areas will be built, listed park buildings will be renovated and garden areas rejuvenated. The Friends of Locke Park organise an annual Easter Fun Day and host a Grand Gala every September.

BRODSWORTH HALL GARDENS
Location: Five miles north-west of Doncaster off A635 Barnsley Road from Junction 37 of A1(M).
Ownership: English Heritage.
Opening Times & Charges: Grounds – beginning of April-end of September: Tuesday-Sunday 12pm-5.30pm; Mondays 11am-4pm. In October Sat. and Sun. only 11am-4pm. Admission for the gardens £4.00; £3.00 concessions and £2.00 children. Visit www.english-heritage.org.uk/yorkshire for special events or telephone 01302 722598.
Facilities: Free parking. Toilets. Gift shop. Tearoom (not Mondays). No dogs.
Special Features: Grade II* listed garden. Fifteen acres of garden laid out shortly after the rebuilding of Brodsworth Hall in the 1860s with ornamental flower beds, nineteenth century roses, an Italianate fountain, statues and sculptures, a quarry garden with ferns including the giant tree fern, *Dicksonia antarctica*. All linked by walks lined with clipped yew, ivy and holly. Vistas. Italianate summerhouse, target house and game larder. Lovely old cedar tree on the east lawn on the approach to the hall.

The formal Italianate gardens looking towards Brodsworth Hall.

Looking across the formal gardens towards the Summer House.

Flower-filled tazza.

Superimposed onto an Earlier Landscape

The Brodsworth estate and its mid-eighteenth century house were acquired by Peter Thellusson, a banker, in about 1790. In an extraordinary will he left it and the rest of his fortune to accumulate for three generations.[1] Charles Sabine Augustus Thellusson (1822-85) inherited the estate in 1859 and decided to build a new house. Chevalier Casentini designed the house in the Italianate style. It was built and furnished in only three years (1861-63) with the building work being undertaken by London architect Philip Wilkinson.[2] The gardens were laid out between 1863 and 1870. Old buildings and hedges were removed, new drives made, trees and shrubs planted and garden buildings constructed. Between 1865 and 1867 Casentini provided a large number of marble ornaments for the garden including eight greyhound sculptures.

In 1931 the estate was inherited by Charles Thelluson's grandson, Charles Grant-Dalton and it was his daughter, Pamela Williams, who gave the house and gardens to English Heritage in 1990. By this time the house and its contents were in a perilous state of decay and the gardens were overgrown. After a five year programme of restoration and conservation Brodsworth Hall was opened to the public. Work on the grounds is continuing to this day and the gardens are now a joy to behold.

The Garden Experience

The main drive sweeps up through parkland and swings through lawns and shrubberies to the east front of the house. The main pleasure grounds lie to the west of the house. Neat lawns surround the house which sits on a raised terrace of grass banks. Because herbicides have not been used on the lawns they are valuable remnants of magnesian limestone grassland, rich in wild flowers such as milkwort, rock rose, thyme, cowslip and orchid. Twelve shallow urns (tazzas), planted to provide splashes of colour, and eight marble greyhounds punctuate the formality around the terrace.

Immediately to the west of the house are croquet lawns and beyond them a large formal garden of symmetrical beds cut out of the turf in shapes that are said to have

55

The Target House.

been unchanged since they were laid out in the 1860s.[3] The patterns for most of the shapes can be found in *The Gardener's Assistant* of 1859. At each corner of this area are four shallow marble urns packed with flowers and in the centre of the garden is a three-tiered marble fountain. It is hoped that water will soon flow again from this impressive fountain. This area exudes colour with traditional bedding formations much loved by the Victorians. Research and care have been taken to use period-correct plants in these schemes. Rising high within this garden are two fine monkey puzzle trees. Many of the evergreen shrubs around this formal planting are tightly clipped into neat shapes with topiary in places.

Beyond this area is the quarry garden known as 'The Grove'. This formed part of the eighteenth century garden but was replanted in the Victorian period. It is an area of intersecting paths, tunnels, steps, banks and bridges. One of its features is the fern dell with the largest collection of hardy ferns in the north of England. Other interesting plants in the dell are geraniums, dwarf conifers, ornamental grasses and tree ferns. A quiet trickle of water, bordered by primulas, descends through a rocky stepped channel and a 'river' of pale gravel traverses the floor of this sheltered dell. Joseph Barron (thought to be a son of William Barron of Elvaston Nurseries, the Victorian garden designer) received payment for some of the rock work in this area in 1864. High on a mound is a classical stone summerhouse built in 1866 and recently restored. Behind this is the pets' cemetery with about twenty graves.

Along the western edge of the gardens is the target range, a long open space once flanked by formal iris borders, where the family and their friends could practise archery.[4] Along here there are now some interesting trees including three *Ginkgo biloba* trees. At its northern end is the Target House, a small garden building, built in a rustic Swiss style in the 1860s. This building houses a small, interesting exhibition about the history of the gardens. At the other end of this open pathway is an 'eyecatcher' – in this case, the façade of a building halfway up a cliff! Just beyond the Target House is a formal rose garden with clipped box hedges and a central curved iron pergola covered in roses and vines. The roses are mainly nineteenth century varieties.

On-going work in the woodland area to the north of the house includes tree surgery to open up areas of dense shade. Near the old game larder are a few Strawberry trees, *Arbutus unedo* and *andrachnoides*, which have lychee-like fruits in October and ripen to a rich strawberry red. English Heritage (and the garden staff) need to be commended for all their efforts in bringing this garden back to its former splendour. After your exertions around the garden's many acres, tea and scones can be recommended at the tearoom.

CANNON HALL, PARK AND GARDENS
Location: Near Cawthorne, 3 miles north-west of Barnsley off the A635.
Ownership: Barnsley Metropolitan Borough Council.
Opening times & charges: Open all year round. Entrance to the park and gardens is free.
Facilities: Ample parking in pay-and-display car parks, Cannon Hall Museum (01226 790270), garden centre with café, Cannon Hall Farm café, gift shop, farm shop, open farm.
Special features: 70 acres of historic parkland, serpentine river with cascades and bridges, formal gardens, magnificent walled garden with historic pear collection and glasshouses.

John Spencer's Legacy
The landscape that we see around Cannon Hall today is largely the legacy of John Spencer (1718-1775), a lawyer and MP, whose family had achieved wealth through their involvement in the iron trades of the district. The history of the estate can be traced back to the fourteenth century when Thomas de Bosvile was owner and received a grant of free warren from the king in 1381. Little more is known until 1650 when 'the manor, farm and capital messuage called Cannon Hall' were conveyed from William Hewet to Robert Hartley. Shortly afterwards John Spencer (d.1681) married Robert Hartley's widow and purchased the estate from the Hartley family.[1] The Spencer family (becoming Spencer Stanhope in 1775, when John Spencer left the estate to his nephew Walter Stanhope, who took the name Walter Spencer Stanhope) held the Cannon Hall estate until it was sold to Barnsley Council in 1951. The house opened as a museum in 1957.

When John Spencer inherited the Cannon Hall estate from his father in 1756 he set about remodelling and extending the house, employing John Carr, the York architect, to add two one-storey wings to the central part of the house (his nephew subsequently added a second floor to the two wings and in the Victorian period a further wing was added). He also re-designed the gardens and parkland. Many of John Spencer's diaries and eighteenth century lists of trees and plants for Cannon Hall are in Sheffield Archives. His diaries depict an energetic bachelor, passionate about hunting with frequent notes such as 'the hounds were out, killed a Brace of Hares'[2] and 'foxhunting killed an old dog Fox.'[3] He often made visits to London and whether at home or away he rarely seemed to dine alone, when at home, usually with gentry friends from the neighbourhood. The enthusiasm for the development of his house and parkland is also evident and he was keen to impress.

An oil painting of the park at Cannon Hall looking towards Cawthorne church. Courtesy Cannon Hall Museum

The Grand Plan

It appears that all did not go well initially with his garden plans – on 5 January 1757 he optimistically wrote 'out shooting in the morning and afternoon Henry Bolton my new Gardener came this Day'. By August he had dismissed Bolton – 'Discharg'd Henry Bolton my Gardener for occasioning Disturbances amongst and raising false Reports of other Servants.'[4] By 1760, however, plans were afoot for a grand scheme. John Spencer engaged Richard Woods, a nurseryman and landscape architect from Chertsey in Surrey, to re-design the parkland around Cannon Hall. The diary is peppered with references to Mr Woods – 'Mr Woods … here this morning … laying out Grounds all Day'[5] and many which simply state 'At Home with Mr Woods.'[6] The plan made by Richard Woods in 1760 can be seen in Sheffield Archives and it shows a new walled kitchen garden, a pinery and hot-house and the park with trees and shrubs. Deer were introduced into the park and the water course (the Daking Brook) was altered and broadened with pools and cascades created. Bridges were constructed along the river's course.

The Hot House and Pinery

In 1760 work began apace. Terms were agreed with Mr Teal, a carpenter, and Mr Dodgson and Mr Bower, bricklayers, to undertake the construction of the kitchen garden walls and the building of the hot house and pinery. Mr Williams, a brickmaker, was 'to make the Bricks for me upon the same Terms he made for Sir William Wentworth [of Bretton Hall].'[7] John Spencer was obviously keen to share the plans for the improvements of his estate with his gentry friends and neighbours. On 18 April 1760 he wrote 'Sir William Wentworth, Mr Phipps and Mr West din'd here, shewed Sir William Wentworth the proposed alterations which he approvd'.

The hot house and pinery were completed on time, being 'reared' in August 1760. The next month 'Thomas Peach, Mr Woods Man'[8] arrived to work at Cannon Hall and on 25 September John Spencer 'Wrote to Lord Strafford for Pine Apple Plants.' He also acquired pineapple plants from Sir William Wentworth and eighty from Mr Stanhope (his brother-in-law). On 23 October he proudly wrote 'cut the first Pine Apple out of my Hot House.' A list of hot-house plants for 1761 survives recording a most exotic selection of fifty-seven stove plants including a 'Coffe tree … Chinese periwinkle … Double Oleander … Canary Campanula … Persian Cyclamen … Sweet Smelling Cape Lily … Jacobea Amarillis … Aloe [and] Black Egyptian Arum.'[9] In front of the hot house and pinery Richard Woods' plan shows a semi-circular area known as the balloon 'to be richly adorned with the choicest flowers & low exoticks.' The walls of the hot house remain but it is now roofless. The area in front of the hot house now boasts smart geometrically shaped flower beds set in lawns and crammed with bulbs and bedding plants. To the east of the walled garden is now the so-called 'fairyland,' a wilderness with rhododendrons, a fish-pond (the remains of the medieval fish ponds?), and stone masonry thought to have come from Cawthorne church when it was being renovated in the nineteenth century.

Looking across the formal gardens towards the hot house and pinery.

The Walled Kitchen Garden

A walled kitchen garden existed at Cannon Hall prior to John Spencer's time though it appears to have been in a different location because he wrote in his diary on 9 April 1760 'Fix'd a Place for a new Kitchen Garden.' There are lists of fruit trees for 1719, 1732 and 1735, the latter recording peaches, nectarines, apricots, pears and cherries planted for William Spencer by John Perfect of Pontefract.

Glasshouses within the walled kitchen garden.

The list of fruit trees for the Cannon Hall walled kitchen garden for 1761[10] is amazing. There are fourteen different types of peach, including 'Smiths Newington, Royal George and French Mignion'; six kinds of nectarine; six varieties of apricot; eight different cherries; sixteen varieties of 'plumbs' including 'Red Queen Mother, Drab Dore, and St Catherine'; five types of pears ('Chaumontelle, Virgolue, Colmar, St German and Crusade') and eleven vines including White and Black Muscadine. Since the eighteenth century there have been changes to the types of fruit tree in the garden. Today Cannon Hall is noted for its historic pear collection with around forty different varieties of dessert pear. It is one of the most extensive collections in the north of England. Some are thought to be almost 200 years old. They include Laxton's Superb, Doyenne du Comice and Jargonelle. Most of the trees are trained against the brick walls as espaliers. There are also two peaches, one nectarine, one cherry, three

The 200-year-old vine in the vinery in the kitchen garden.

plums, one vine and seven apple trees. A booklet, *The Historic Pear Collection*, can be purchased in the sales area of the museum.

The best clue regarding the types and range of vegetables grown comes from a list of 1816, when vegetable seeds were purchased from Oxley, Thomas and Scholey.[11] Walter Spencer Stanhope bought three types of onion, two spinach, three radish, one carrot and one turnip, five varieties of lettuce, some scorzonera seeds, some salsify, two types of cabbage, beetroot, five different kinds of peas and some broccoli seeds. He also ordered some parsley seeds, cucumber, balsam and mallow.

The glasshouses that are in the walled garden have been adapted and rebuilt over the years. The northern range has a central area which was once the display house filled with flowering plants for the family and their guests to enjoy. The glasshouses on either side were for figs, vines, peaches, nectarines and apricots. The (now bricked up) archways were for grapes which had their roots outside and their branches inside. The sheds at the back of this range included a mushroom and forcing house, a Robin Hood Senior boiler, a fuel store and a tool shed. The garden mess room to the east was apparently used until 1960. The southern glasshouse range has a hot wall for growing vines against (even visible on the 1760 plan). The account of work completed kept by George Swift for Walter Spencer Stanhope in 1805[12] demonstrates the importance of good maintenance. Swift receives payment for 'cleaning the flues of the stoves in the garden', for 'laying [the] causeway in the Garden' and for 'pointing the stoves and Repairing the walls of the vinery'.

Amongst the garden accounts is one for 1794 for work done by William Smith, a tailor. He received payment for a variety of tasks including 'Mend'g Breeches, Mend'g Coat & Waistcoate, Mend'g Fustian Jacket and Mak'g Coat and Waistcoate.[13] Did the gardeners have to wear some type of livery?

The Park

John Marsden, a mason, was employed for a number of years from 1760 building (or re-building) the park wall and 'Ha ha digging', constructing bridges, dams and cascades in the river 'achler [ashlar] work at the cascade' and building gateways including a 'Gate Way by [the] Pleasure Ground.'[14] Once the park wall was intact the landscaping of the park and stocking with deer could begin in earnest. On 20 January 1762 John Spencer wrote 'At Home, setting out Plantations in the Park.' In February the first deer arrived. He wrote 'Strong Frost and Rime. The Gamekeeper returned from Sprodborough with twenty Bucks.'[15] Two days later he noted that 'Mr Radcliffe & Mr Brooks came here with the Deer from Sir George Armytages [of Kirk Lees Hall]' and on 6 February 'Mr Radcliffe & Mr Phipps & myself went to Gunthwaite, took the deer out of Gunthwaite Park & put them into my Park.' In the week beginning the 1 February 1762 John Spencer noted 'Number of Deer put into my Park this week … 89.' The present deer shed is a nineteenth century replacement in 'gothic' style. At the end of the nineteenth century there were still over 100 fallow deer in the park but the last ones disappeared over fifty years ago.

The planting of trees continued for a number of years evidenced by diary entries such as 'Planted … Oaks, Elms, Beech, Firrs, Chestnuts…'[16] 'A very Foggy misling day planting & staking with Mr Woods'[17] and 'Planted large Trees in the Park.'[18] Another eighteenth century list has been deposited in Sheffield Archives[19] of trees and shrubs for Cannon Hall. It includes 'Triplethorn Acatia, dwarf almonds, mountain ash, cistus, Red Virginia Cedars, four Cedar of Lebanon, eleven types of honeysuckle, striped hollies, two Scarlet flower Maples, six American Scarlet Oak, two double pomegranates, 210 Laurel trees, Plumb and twenty dwarf Laburnums'. Today the trees in the parkland are a pleasure at any season.

The Serpentine River

It appears that work began on the alterations to Daking Brook on 26 October 1761 with 'the making of the new bridge'. Pools were created joined by cascades which were built of horizontally bedded stone-slabs to give a natural effect. On 22 June 1762 John Spencer wrote 'At Home with Mr Woods setting out the Piece of Water below the Bridge.' Later in the year he noted 'At Home. Planting in the Park saw the cascade play for the first time.'[20] In February 1764 he 'signed a Contract with Mr Woods whereby he engages to complete my next Piece of Water & ... make a Palladian Bridge and a Head at the Park Wall to raise the Water for 330 ft to be compleat in twenty weeks Time.'[21] He showed the developments to his nephew, Walter Stanhope in January 1765 stating 'Frosty & foggy. Went over the Grounds with Watty.'[22] In March 1765 he ordered two boats and on 9 July of that year after a spell in London you can almost feel the pleasure when he wrote 'At Home all day sailing and fishing.'

Looking across the serpentine lake towards Cannon Hall.

Pears; Beurre de Jonghe, Doyenne du Comice and Emile D'Heyst. Robert Thompson, The Gardener's Assistant, Vol 4, 1901

CLUMBER PARK AND WALLED KITCHEN GARDEN

Location: 4¹/₂ miles south-east of Worksop, 6¹/₂ miles south-west of Retford.

Ownership: National Trust.

Opening times and charges: Park open all year during daylight hours. Kitchen garden: end of March – end of October on Wednesdays, Thursdays & Fridays 10am–5.30pm and Saturdays, Sundays & BH Mondays 10am-6pm. Phone 01909 476592 for further details. Admission to the park is free but there is a vehicle charge of £3.80 per car. Admission to the kitchen garden is £1.00, members free.

Facilities: Tearoom/restaurant, shop, toilets. Powered vehicles & wheelchairs for the disabled – pre-book via the estate office. Fishing, orienteering, etc.

Special features: 3,800 acres of parkland (with 2,000 acres of peaceful woods, open heath and rolling farmland); a two-mile long serpentine lake and avenue of limes. Over 1,000 acres of the park are protected under SSSI status. Historic lodges & gateways. Eighteenth century lakeside temple. Eighteenth century walled kitchen garden open to the public as a working example of a nineteenth century kitchen garden with a vinery, palm house and museum. For special events and talks visit the website: www.nationaltrust.org.uk.

Clumber House, Park and Pleasure Grounds

Listed in the Domesday Survey of 1086 as 'Clunbre' the park took its present shape in the early eighteenth century when the land was acquired by the Dukes of Newcastle.[1] Initially it was a hunting park with a lodge and around 400 red deer. From the second half of the eighteenth century there were enormous changes. In the 1760s large numbers of trees were planted – beech, chestnut, willow, elm and Cedars of Lebanon and work began on creating a serpentine lake from the River Poulter crossed by a Palladian bridge, and a mansion, Clumber House, was built around the old hunting lodge to designs by Stephen Wright.[2] In the 1770s the kitchen garden was initiated with a vinery and other stoves and in the 1780s the lakeside temple was built. Park lodges and gateways were also constructed.

In 1817 the lake was deepened and there were boats on it. By 1821 the Duke even employed a sailor to look after them![3] A grotto was being made in the 1820s but, according to the Duke, 'some mischievous and evil spirited people went to the new Grotto … and broke off the shells carrying some away and leaving others on the ground.'[4] In the same period Robert Smirke and William Sawrey Gilpin collaborated to design spectacular terraced gardens between the mansion and the lake. One of the finest features in the park – the Lime Avenue, the longest in Europe – dates from about 1840. Planted by the 4th Duke of Newcastle it is almost two miles long and consists of a double row of lime trees (*Tilia x europea*) – 1,296 in total.

As with many country estates there were periods of plenty and times of financial insecurity. In 1879 fire swept through the core of Clumber House but it was rebuilt to a design by Charles Barry, whose father and namesake had designed the Houses of Parliament. Its heyday was probably the end of the nineteenth century and the first two decades of the twentieth century. There were royal visits and extravagant entertaining and even locals were allowed to take charabanc trips to admire the splendour of the park. These halcyon days were however doomed.[5] After the economic slump of the 1920s the park went into decline with silver birch and rhododendrons invading the area. The contents of the house were dispersed and in 1937 there was a week-long grand sale of the contents including fireplaces, marble staircases, balustrades and even bricks. Magnificent garden ornaments were also sold. In 1938 the house itself was demolished. Visitors can now only trace the outline of the Palladian house. The National Trust purchased Clumber Park in 1946.

The Walled Kitchen Garden

The eighteenth century walls enclose about four acres of garden. At one time a further six acres of the surrounding area would also have been under cultivation so that the family could be self-sufficient in fruit and vegetables. In the early 1900s there were twenty-nine full-time gardeners – now there are three! Assisted by a group of volunteers the kitchen garden has been brought back from near dereliction. Both traditional and modern growing techniques are used and the garden is completely organic.

The Long Range of glasshouses in the kitchen garden.

Exhibits in the kitchen garden museum:

(a) bottles used in the storage of grapes
*(b) leather shoes for covering horses' hooves
when cutting lawns or walking on cinder paths*
(c) old tools.

Along the northern wall is a magnificent glasshouse known as the Long Range dating from 1908. This is the only glasshouse to survive. It is 450 feet long and actually comprises twelve distinct glasshouses. The western range contains figs and four varieties of dessert grape including Black Hamburgh and Buckland Sweetwater. On the eastern side nectarines and peaches grow alongside sweet corn, chillies, melons, tomatoes, cucumbers, courgettes and aubergines. The central Conservatory and Palm House are magnificent with flowering plants such as daturas, fuchsias, pelargoniums and abutilons.

Along the outside of the north wall is an assortment of garden buildings – once potting sheds, mushroom houses and storerooms. They now house the garden museum with a splendid array of old tools – scythes, spades, forks, rakes, hoes, secateurs and even ancient lawnmowers. One area shows a typical mess room in a gardeners' bothy. There are copies of old seed catalogues, leather shoes for horses (so that they didn't spoil the lawns or garden paths) and specially shaped bottles designed to store grapes for months. Beneath this area are water storage tanks that collect rainwater from the rooftops. This is then recycled through the irrigation system in the garden.

The path that runs south from the conservatory towards the main garden gates is bordered by herbaceous beds which look their best in July and August, being planted in 'hot' colours. On either side of the herbaceous borders are the vegetable plots. On one side are over seventy pre-1910 varieties of vegetables such as 'Red Drumhead'

Cordon-grown apples.

cabbages, Brussels sprouts, 'Green Topped Scotch' turnips, parsnips, strawberries, carrots, kohl rabi and even scorzonera 'Black Giant of Russia'. On the opposite side of the main path are modern varieties. The apple orchard was established in 1985 and along with wall-trained fruit includes fifty-eight varieties that are from Nottinghamshire and surrounding counties such as Sissons Worksop Newton, Bess Pool and Bramley's Seedling.[6]

Along the western wall, on the site of glasshouses specifically for growing carnations, is a herb border. Here are tuberous nasturtiums, spearmint, fennel, borage, red orache, horseradish, oca, racambole, sage, lovage and marjoram to name but a few.

On leaving the walled garden look to the right to see the attractive red-brick Head Gardener's house built in 1892 (now a private residence) and beyond that, to the right, the gardeners' bothy (now the estate office). There are several Fruit and Vegetable Tasting Days each year when visitors can sample unusual fruit and vegetables, try delicious recipes and compare the flavour of traditional and modern varieties.

Tasting Day at Clumber kitchen garden.

CUSWORTH HALL AND PARK

Location: Cusworth Lane, Doncaster, off the A638 Wakefield to Doncaster Road.
Ownership: Doncaster Metropolitan Borough Council.
Opening Times & Charges: Cusworth Hall (now the Museum of South Yorkshire Life) and grounds open Mon-Fri 10am – 5pm; Sat 11am-5pm; Sun 11am-5pm (4pm in January & December). Admission is free. Tel: 01302 782342. Website: www.doncaster.gov.uk/museums.
Facilities: Car parking. Tearoom, museum shop.
Special features: A Richard Woods' landscape of the 1760s with lakes, a cascade and a grotto-like boathouse. It is undergoing a major restoration supported by a £7.3m grant from the Heritage Lottery Fund and Doncaster Council. It is hoped that work will be completed by 2006.

Cusworth and its Hall

Place-name evidence suggests an Anglo-Saxon origin for the settlement of Cusworth, *Cuthsa's enclosure*, and an early fourteenth century document mentions a 'capital messuage' (large house) at Cusworth.[1] The family associated with the present house and its parkland from 1669 until 1961 were the Wrightsons who became the Battie-Wrightsons. William Wrightson (1676-1760) was the owner responsible for the building of the hall that stands today and for initiating changes to the grounds.

Between 1726 and 1735 William Wrightson enlarged the gardens by building high brick and stone walls to contain a bowling green, flower garden, hall garden, greenhouse garden, kitchen garden, a lower garden called Low Piece and an orchard.[2] These became known as the Walled Gardens. In 1726 he built a summer house (which became the Bowling Pavilion). Foundations for the present hall were dug in 1740 and the previous hall dismantled, some materials being used in the construction of other buildings such as the Head Gardener's house and a bothy. George Platt, the Rotherham mason-architect, was responsible for the initial work on

Looking across the serpentine lake towards Cusworth Hall from a hand-coloured steel engraving, 1831.

the new hall and on his death in 1742 his son John took over the contract. William Wrightson was apparently extremely keen to keep a watchful eye on the building work and it is alleged that, 'from a bosun's chair fixed to the scaffolding of the partly constructed house, he daily gave instructions and supervision'.[3] On completion of the central hall, William's son-in-law, John Battie, said that he considered it was 'too tall for its length' and consequently it was proposed to add two wings. The design for these was given to James Paine, the Palladian-style architect. Between 1750-55 various master craftsmen were involved with work on the interiors including Joseph Rose, noted for his stucco plasterwork, and artist Francis Hayman, once a student of Hogarth, who painted the *Good Samaritan* picture and *The Ascension* scene on the vaulted ceiling of the chapel. The hall was completed in 1755 with costs amounting to £20,000.

The 'Naturalistic' Parkland

It was John Battie (who married Isabella Wrightson, the only surviving child and heiress of William) who commissioned Richard Woods, the landscape gardener from Chertsey in Surrey, to make improvements to the 100 acre grounds around the new Cusworth Hall in 1761. Woods produced plans and memoranda for the creation of a 'naturalistic' landscaped park at Cusworth to be supervised by his foreman, Thomas Colia (spelt in various ways).

There are precise instructions for digging ('grubbing up'), earth moving, tree planting, hedge laying, the making of gravel walkways and coach roads and the construction of the lakes, a bridge, a grotto-like boathouse and a cascade. Richard Woods marked out his design with the aid of numbered stakes. Thomas Colia was

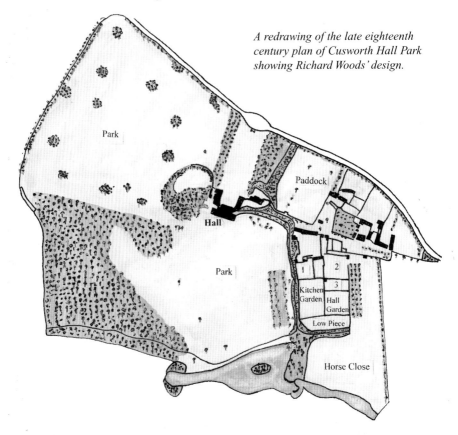

A redrawing of the late eighteenth century plan of Cusworth Hall Park showing Richard Woods' design.

given instructions for all aspects of the work including what and where to plant in detailed memoranda exemplified by the following:

> *Stake No 3 is the Center of a Clump wch may be about 60 yards Long. The middle of which for 20 yards Should be Deciduous plants and Each End firrs, but of Different Sorts for Example one End may be Scotch & the other Spruce or any Other two Sorts, and In front of this Clump Plant larches for 25 yards Long.*[4]

Woods selected existing trees, where suitably placed in clumps within the park, to furnish the new landscape thus giving an immediate 'maturity'. He was keen that his plans were followed meticulously, informing Colia that 'a great deal [is] to be observed, and [that] great Care must be taken to Exicute it properly'.[5] A wide variety of trees were planted in clumps and open groves – cypress, red cedar, beech, elm, chestnut, larch, tulip, fir and pine interspersed with evergreens and underplanted with roses and honeysuckle intended to grow amongst them.

In creating the 'naturalistic' landscape a large amount of time and money were spent on the formation of a concave-convex slope between the hall and the artificial lakes. Colia was told 'to work the lawn … in a gentle Concave Slope from the top line of the Stakes Down to the lower line and then Reverse it to a Convex, for a Considerable Space, and then fall into the natural Concave below down to the river'.[6] What a task with little or no mechanisation! Woods insisted in having the ground dug 'about 2 spitt [spade lengths] deep where the Plough Cannot go'[7] to give the trees and shrubs a good start.

After the levelling, planting and turfing came the construction, between February 1763 and November 1764, of three lakes, formed from the stream called Rose Dyke. A boathouse, designed as an arch, was to give the effect of a cave hidden among the thick foliage. The individual sections of the arch were made of artificial 'stone' produced from a mould to look 'very rough and shaggy'. Woods told Colia to 'cover the top of the arch with Earth' to make it resemble 'a Natural Swelling Hill' plant it with fir trees and position a seat 'at least 15 feet Back from the front of the arch'.[8] Between the upper water or 'Great River' and the middle pond a cascade was built to give the impression of a natural rugged waterfall.

The grotto-like boathouse.

Fallow deer had grazed the old park at Cusworth and Woods instructed that the plantings should be protected from the deer by putting stakes about nine feet high all round the clumps and running two or three rows of rope round them so that the deer could not creep under.[9] Deer remained at Cusworth until the Second World War when they disappeared one night after the park gates were left open.[10]

An indication of eighteenth century planting can be obtained from an order, supplied by J and G Perfect of Pontefract, to Cusworth in 1785 totalling £7-5s-7d.[11] Trees and shrubs purchased include birch, 'Lord Weymouth' pines, viburnum, laurel, lilac, box, acacia, juniper, '2 South Sea Thea trees', almond, holly, pyracantha, guelder rose and sea buckthorn. Flowering plants obtained were jasmine, hypericum, myrtle, honeysuckle, lychnidea, cinquefoil and roses. Thirteen types of apple trees, four kinds of cherry trees, eight types of pears and four species of plums were, no doubt, destined for the kitchen garden.

Two Hundred Years on
The basic layout, designed by Richard Woods, changed little over the next two centuries and the same family, becoming the Battie-Wrightsons, owned the hall and its grounds. As with many country estates, the commissioning of the estate by the military during the Second World War severely disrupted maintenance. When Robert Battie-Wrightson, the last squire to live at Cusworth, died in 1952 the hall was in a dilapidated state. With heavy death duties to be paid, the contents of the hall were sold at auction in October of that year. The building and its grounds were eventually purchased by Doncaster R D C in 1961 for £7,500 and it became a museum in 1967. Ownership transferred to Doncaster M B C in 1974 and the museum's theme became South Yorkshire life.

A sweet chestnut tree.

Dredging the serpentine lake in September 2004.

Revival

The grant from the Heritage Lottery Fund, supported by Doncaster MBC, is breathing new life into both Cusworth Hall Museum and its eighteenth century designed landscape. Work on the grounds commenced at the beginning of 2004 with the felling of trees and the clearing of overgrown shrubberies. The water features (lakes, cascade, bridge and boathouse) and the parkland, designed by Richard Woods in the 1760s, are being restored to reflect his original concept and the fashion of the time. Great care is being taken at every stage to protect the wildlife within the park. Paths, benches and car parking facilities are to be upgraded also. A garden terrace is to be created near the hall in a style typical of the early twentieth century. The old walled kitchen garden (to which there is no public access at present) is to have its walls repaired. Additional funding will be needed to restore the area within the walls – the bowling green, the kitchen garden and the orchard. The eighteenth century summer house/bowling pavilion survives near the old bowling green. It would be wonderful to see this area returned to its former uses to complete the picture of how the estate operated in the past. South Yorkshire does not have an eighteenth century bowling green (and only one working kitchen garden) and this area, once restored, could be a unique feature if it too could be funded.

DONCASTER'S URBAN PUBLIC PARKS

Doncaster is the exception among the four major urban centres in South Yorkshire in that it does not have a Victorian public park as such. In 1896 recreation for Doncaster's population was provided in Sandall Beat Wood, a plantation in which paths, picnic areas, swings and a shelter were provided. Elmfield Park did not come into existence until the 1920s and Hexthorpe Flatts did not officially become a park until 1928. The borough's lack of historic urban parks is compensated for by the landscape park at nearby Cusworth Hall, which is in local authority ownership, and by English Heritage's Brodsworth Hall Gardens.

ELMFIELD PARK

Location: Half a mile to the south-east of Doncaster town centre.

Facilities: Bowling greens, multi-use playgrounds; children's play area.

Special features: Rose garden, attractive flower beds with some carpet bedding, remains of a fountain now planted with flowers, war memorial by the main gates along South Parade.

Private estate to people's park

Around 1803 Colonel John Walbanke Childers, owner of Cantley Hall and the Carr House estate, built the elegant Elmfield House. It is thought to have been built as a dower house for his widowed mother, Sarah. Following her death in 1817 it was occupied by several tenants until it was bought by the Jarrett family in 1853. In 1920 Ellen Charlotte Jarrett sold the house and twenty-eight acres of land to Doncaster Corporation for £30,000 for use as a public park.[1] The Corporation had come under criticism for not acquiring other estates for use as public parks for the people of Doncaster apparently because they thought 'that the Race Common provided the townsfolk with adequate means of recreation.'[2]

Looking towards the war memorial from Elmfield Park.

The Borough engineer (with no previous experience) designed the park with its many pathways and flower beds. In 1923 the war memorial was unveiled at the main entrance to the park and in 1925 the dolphin fountain was created. Recollections from park users recall the bandstand (and dancing around it to music provided by a gramophone), the children's paddling pool and the recreation area with its 'ranty-shanty.'[3] The park is still planted with attractive bedding (and carpet bedding) and is well-used. Elmfield House is currently the headquarters of Doncaster Borough Youth Service.

HEXTHORPE FLATTS

Location: South-west of Doncaster town centre at Hexthorpe.

Facilities: Bowling green, children's play area, walks along tree-lined pathways, flower beds.

Special features: Bandstand, some interesting trees, remains of 'The Dell', a planted old quarry.

From Quarry to Park

The first documentary evidence of quarrying at Hexthorpe dates from 1568.[1] The rock, Upper Magnesian Limestone, was referred to as 'slate' because, being thinly bedded, it could be split easily and used as roofing slates. It was also used as walling material. An example of the stone can be seen by examining the park gate posts, built in 1929. Quarrying continued until the nineteenth century.

Ginkgo tree at Hexthorpe Flatts.

Official council minutes show that the Corporation were considering Hexthorpe Flatts 'for the purpose of laying out and planting as a public pleasure ground' in 1850.[2] Joseph Paxton was approached but suggested that the Corporation ought to consider other priorities – a cemetery and improvement to the water works!

It was June 1902 before the idea for a public park at Hexthorpe was resurrected. The sum of £250 was allocated for sloping the quarry walls, making a tea-house, building a bandstand, providing toilets and planting willows. On August Bank Holiday of that year the grounds were opened to the public for the first time with the Doncaster Temperance Band providing the music.[3] The following year saw further planting of trees and the issuing of a contract to Mrs H Anderson to provide boats for hire on the River Don. The River Don forms the western boundary of the park and boating became so popular that a boathouse was built alongside the river in 1904.

Bandstand in The Dell at Hexthorpe Flatts.

G T Tuby, of the local fairground family, rented land each August Bank Holiday for his gondolas and swings. A pavilion was built next to the bandstand for concerts but both structures were destroyed by fire in 1909.

The late 1920s saw additional facilities – tennis courts, children's swings and seesaws, bowling greens, new gates, a café and a new bandstand. In 1928 Hexthorpe Flatts officially became a park having previously been called a pleasure or recreation area. It was at this time that the old quarry walls were transformed into 'The Dell' with rockeries, walkways and formal beds. Water once flowed in channels at the foot of the dell with a windmill pumping the water around.

In the 1950s Hexthorpe Flatts staged illuminations when crowds flocked to see the lights. A story from about this time tells of a Balby couple on holiday in Bridlington buying tickets for a mystery tour, only to find themselves admiring Hexthorpe illuminations![4]

FANSHAWE GATE HALL AND GARDENS

Location: Two miles west of Dronfield, Derbyshire. Follow B6054 towards Owler Bar from Holmesfield. Take the first turn right after the *Robin Hood Inn.*
Ownership: Privately owned by John and Cynthia Ramsden.
Opening times & charges: Three Sundays in June and July (11-5). Private visits by appointment in June and July only. Tel: 0114 2890391 or visit the website at www.fanshawegate.org.uk.
Facilities: Parking, teas, plant sales. Admission: £3.50.
Special features: Idyllic stone house, tithe barn, dovecote etc. mainly from the sixteenth century surrounded by cottage-style garden with herbaceous borders, roses, herbs, ferns, topiary, water-features, orchard and a small knot garden – a gem!

The Fanshawes

Fanshawe Gate Hall was owned by the same family – the Fanshawes – from around the thirteenth century until the 1940s. Prior to the sixteenth century the name appears on court rolls as Fanchall and Faunchall (and other variations) and it is not until 1543 that the name appears in its present form when John Fanshawe of Fanshawe Gate was bailiff of Holmesfield Manor.[1] John's elder brother, Henry, was Remembrancer of the Exchequer (debt collector) to Queen Elizabeth I. Nine other members of the Fanshawe family held this office between 1566 and 1716.

Sir Richard Fanshawe and his wife, Lady Ann Fanshawe, are perhaps the most well-known family members nationally. Sir Richard had a brilliant and eventful career as a soldier and diplomat in the reign of Charles I but during the Commonwealth was imprisoned. His fortunes revived after the restoration of Charles II in 1660. Lady Ann wrote her memoirs (later published by family members) which tell of cruel separations, the death of a daughter, 'perils at the sword's point … storms at sea and shipwrecks, painful illness, rough fair and dirty lodgings, ghosts, pomp, pillage [and] plague.'[2]

Succeeding generations had distinguished careers in academic life, the army and navy, the church and the colonial service. The last family member to live at Fanshawe Gate Hall was Althea Fanshawe in the 1740s, after which it became a tenanted farm until it was bought by Richard Genders in 1944. He was followed by the Marrians and then the present owners, John and Cynthia Ramsden, who purchased Fanshawe Gate Hall in 1959.[3]

A Tour of the Garden

The original dwelling, which once stood on or near the site of the existing house, was demolished about 400 years ago. Some of the stone was used in the construction of the present, much smaller building. With walls of rough, thin sandstone strengthened by dressed gritstone quoins and mullions and roofed with stone slates, the house now supports a multitude of climbers including roses (*Rosa* 'Pink Perpetue'), clematis, ceanothus and honeysuckle. It also provides a back-drop for hollyhocks, monkshood, bellflowers, phlox and asters.

Agapanthus.

The one and a half acre garden, at 800 feet above sea level, is cut into an easterly-facing hill on various levels and is divided by stone walls and hedges into different areas. The first glimpse for a visitor is down the driveway to the hall from Fanshawe Gate Lane. At the side of the lane are two gateposts, about fifteen feet high, possibly dating from the sixteenth century. They are made from dressed stone and topped by spherical gritstone finials and hold a pair of wrought iron gates incorporating the Fanshawe coat-of-arms and designed by the Ramsdens. Both sides of the driveway are planted in shades of blue and gold. 'Happy Child' standard roses, *clematis orientalis* and alchemilla provide the gold, and agapanthus, nepeta, lavender and other clematis the shades of blue. Further along the driveway is another pair of old

Stone gateposts at Fanshawe Gate Hall.　　*Topiary and exuberant planting.*

The sixteenth century dovecote.

stone gateposts topped by carved cones/acorns.

On open days visitors can inspect the tithe barn, the ancient ash tree and pond before entering the lower courtyard with its neat box knot garden and mushroom-shaped staddle-stones supporting moss and lichen covered stone beams by the woodland area. Against the cottage wall is a herb border and on the north-eastern side a 'memory' border containing plants that, according to Cynthia Ramsden, 'are treasured gifts or ones that recall happy memories.'[4] This area leads to the Elizabethan garden with its hexagonal summerhouse. The summerhouse was rescued in the 1970s from the garden of Cynthia Ramsden's grandfather. Originally thatched it is now covered with felt roofing tiles. The border on the west of this area is variegated, broken by blocks of bronze-coloured plants. A visitor can then proceed across the driveway to the new wildlife pond, orchard and vegetable garden. Fruit and nut trees that would have been known in the sixteenth century have been planted in the old orchard – walnut, medlar, mulberry and fig.

The area to the south of the house again reflects Cynthia Ramsden's philosophy of 'exuberant planting on the point of bursting into riot, but supported and restrained where necessary to keep some balance and harmony.'[5] This area is a delightful spot with topiary, ferns, astilbe, hostas, roses and the lion waterfall. To the east of the house is a terrace with lawns and borders. These borders have species and cultivars which were known in England in the sixteenth and seventeenth centuries – foxgloves, mullein, aquilegia, campanula, mallow, geranium, dianthus and honesty – to name but a few. From here the potting shed and greenhouse can be inspected. In the south-east corner of the main lawn is the splendid three-storey sixteenth century dovecote, restored in 1991. Further borders contain iris, astilbe and crocosmia with sambucus and cornus – all in prime condition.

Fanshawe Gate Hall and its garden are an inspiration and a delight. Cynthia Ramsden, her family and helpers have created a wonderful garden and are keen to share it with others in June and July each year. Proceeds go to various charities including Macmillan Cancer Relief and the Oesophageal Patients Association.

HODSOCK PRIORY GARDENS
Location: Well signposted off the B6045 at Blyth, north Nottinghamshire, less than two miles from the A1(M).
Ownership: Privately owned by Sir Andrew and Lady Belinda Buchanan. Tel: 01909 591204 or visit the website: www.snowdrops.co.uk.
Opening times & charges: Usually open every day for five weeks from the beginning of February. Admission £4, no concessions. Children (6-16) £1.
Facilities: Ample free parking. Refreshments. Toilets. Plant sales area.
Special features: Garden of five acres with snowdrops, miniature narcissi, cyclamens, hellebores, aconites and winter-flowering shrubs. Woodland of twelve acres, carpeted with snowdrops.

Looking across the lake towards Hodsock Priory.

History

When the Domesday Book was compiled in 1086 the Hodsock estate was farmed by the Saxon, Ulsi, under the Norman lord, Roger de Busli.[1] There has never been a priory here the name 'priory' is purely fictitious, but there was a large moated manor house dating from the middle of the twelfth century when the Cress(e)y family held it.[2] Visitors still approach the gardens via a bridge over the moat which, although dry, still encloses the five acre garden. By the beginning of the fifteenth century the estate had passed to the Cliftons through marriage and it remained with the Clifton family for over 350 years. This family was responsible for building the magnificent brick gatehouse in *c* 1600 with two turrets and a diaper pattern of brickwork. In 1765 Hodsock was sold to the Mellish family, from whom the present owner, Sir Andrew Buchanan, is descended.

The brick house that we see today with its tall, decorated chimneys and diaper brickwork was built in the nineteenth century. The south-west wing is said to be the work of Ambrose Poynter between 1829-33.[3] The remainder of the house was remodelled or rebuilt by George Devey between 1873-76 in Jacobean style to complement the gatehouse. During this period the ornamental gardens were well maintained and 'renowned in the neighbourhood'. A separate walled garden provided the fruit and vegetables for the household.[4]

During the Second World War the Women's Land Army took over the gardens for growing vegetables. In the difficult years after the war tree planting, maintenance and repairs fell behind and when Sir Andrew and Lady Belinda Buchanan took over the 800 acre Hodsock estate in 1966 much work needed to be done.

The Garden and Woodland

After the cold, dark days of December and January it is a sheer delight to walk through the five-acre garden of Hodsock Priory on a mellow February or early March day with the air full of birdsong. The garden consists of lawns, a small lake and a number of water channels with beds and borders crammed with nodding heads of snowdrops, cyclamen, aconites, hellebores, winter and spring flowering shrubs (such as *Prunus cerasi fera* 'Nigra') and bushes whose stems radiate colour (e.g. *Acer conspictuum* 'Phoenix'). Of the mature trees in the garden a century-old *Robina pseudoacacia* (false acacia) is a fine specimen with its sinuous bark and among the more recent plantings the white-barked *Betula jacquemontii* look particularly splendid by the lakeside. In the woodland the swathes of snowdrops are not to be missed.

Hellebores.

The visitor is directed around the garden and woodland along a well-signposted route with numerous garden benches. The wood-chip pathway is wide and mostly flat and allows close inspection of the spring flowers and wide views across the lake back towards the house and gatehouse that reflect in the water. And do look out for the stone sculptures – a frog, tortoise, owl, snail ... and even the tail of a diving whale!

Initially opening on one 'Snowdrop Sunday' in 1990 the garden and woodland are now open every day for a five week period from the beginning of February. Sir Andrew Buchanan's grandmother, Lady Beatrix Stanley, and his parents, Sir Charles and Lady Buchanan, were all keen and talented gardeners and the plant collection has connections with them – for example, *Salvia buchananii* and the snowdrop 'Lady Beatrix Stanley'. For 2003 V-shaped beds were laid out below the terrace, filled with snowdrops and narcissi, to resemble a fan imitating a design from the gardens in the early twentieth century. Another recent innovation is the display of eight working beehives resembling Victorian follies.

Cyclamen and snowdrops growing in profusion.

Snowdrops in the woodland garden.

NOSTELL PRIORY PARK, PLEASURE GROUNDS AND GARDENS

Location: On the A638 five miles south-east of Wakefield towards Doncaster.
Ownership: National Trust.
Opening times & charges: Grounds: end of March – end of October - Wednesday to Sunday 11am-6pm. £2.50. Visit the website for details of other opening times and special events at www.nationaltrust.org.uk.
Facilities: Car parking, shop, tearoom, plant sales, toilets. Powered mobility vehicles and manual wheelchairs, booking essential. Croquet and giant chess.
Special features: Grade II listed park of 346 acres. Lakeside walk, boathouse, and lodges designed by Robert Adam, rose garden, menagerie house, cock pit, gothic arch. Awarded £4.2 million by the Heritage Lottery Fund in November 2002.

From Priory to Mansion

Nostell Priory takes its name from the twelfth century Augustinian priory, dedicated to St Oswald, that once stood on a site just to the south-west of the present house. In 1540, at the Dissolution of the Monasteries, the last prior, Robert Ferror, surrendered the priory to the Crown. The monastic buildings were converted into a dwelling house and later remodelled into a manor house known as 'Nostall Hall'. It was purchased by the Winn family in 1654 and is still lived in by Lord St Oswald, a direct descendant.

Sir Rowland Winn (4th Baronet) began to build the present house and lay out the parkland around it in the 1730s. The house was designed by James Moyser, an enthusiast of Andrea Palladio. The work on the house was undertaken by James Paine (on and off apparently) for the next thirty years. When Sir Rowland Winn (5th Baronet) inherited in 1765 he commissioned Robert Adam to complete the interior in the neo-classic style. Adam also designed the south and west ranges of the stables, the menagerie house and the lodges in the park. There were some nineteenth century additions and renovation work by both Charles Winn (1795-1874) and Rowland Winn (1820-1893). It was conveyed to the National Trust in lieu of tax in 1953 following occupation by the army in the Second World War.[1]

Deer Park to Landscaped Park

Some 200 acres of land surrounding the house were enclosed as a deer park in 1604 – King James I issuing the right of free warren to the Gargraves, the owners of the Nostell estate at that time. It centred on Park Wood which survives as an area of early wood pasture. The estate had farms, woodlands and a medieval fishpond, the latter forming the basis for the Middle Lake we see today. Between 1730 and 1820 the parkland was completely redesigned to provide a setting appropriate for the impressive new house built by Sir Rowland Winn (4th Baronet) and his son.

When the 4th Baronet returned from his Grand Tour in 1729 he commissioned two plans for the grounds at Nostell – one from Stephen Switzer and the other from Joseph Perfect. It seems that Switzer's plan was the one preferred, but even Switzer's design was only partially implemented as far as we know. It showed broad avenues, areas of woodland, garden buildings, winding walks and pieces of water. Near the house his plan showed a formal arrangement of courts and parterres but plans for the lakes had a more naturalistic profile.[2] The avenue of trees, originally of elm but now of sycamore, that forms the long vista to the east of the house may be a legacy of either Switzer's design or Perfect's plan because both show a similar feature. Such tree-lined vistas combined both beauty and utility (in the form of timber production).[3] In the late 1750s the 4th Baronet started to develop the parkland in more of a naturalistic style replacing any earlier formal designs – hence the difficulty of ascertaining how much of Switzer's plan was implemented. In 1759 he created the Upper Lake and planted trees and shrubs to the south of the house and between 1759-61 he also reconstructed the bridge on the Doncaster to Wakefield road to a design by George Savile.[4]

The Middle Lake at Nostell Priory.

The boathouse on the Lower Lake.

The 5th Baronet diverted the Doncaster-Wakefield road and built a high perimeter wall with splendid lodges, designed by Robert Adam. The most impressive lodge, built in 1776, is by the Pontefract to York road. Known as the 'Needle's Eye' this pyramid-shaped Obelisk Lodge has two rooms on either side occupied by keepers until the 1950s. It is currently undergoing restoration. An entrance lodge at Foulby, once ornamented with winged sphinxes, has been demolished and a third gateway, Wragby Lodge, is visible from the church.[5] In the early nineteenth century there was a major planting scheme by James Hank & Co of Keighley with belts and clumps of trees and perimeter woodland in the style of 'Capability' Brown. Additional plantings later in the century were to provide cover for game birds, the Winn family being keen on country sports. A herd of deer grazed in the park for almost four centuries until 1975 after which some of the land was converted to arable farming. The recent award from the Heritage Lottery Fund enabled the National Trust to acquire this land. The Trust plans to restore the area to its historic status as parkland and open up new areas for public access.

The Lower Lake, now managed by a fishing syndicate for large carp, is crossed by a bridge built in 1794 by local architect, Charles Watson. He is also responsible for building the boathouse in this area (also undergoing restoration). The 5th Baronet is said to have owned a six-oared barge with a gilded figure head of Neptune and four small cannon![6]

The Pleasure Grounds and Gardens

Visitors can take a pleasant lakeside walk around the Middle Lake which is managed for wildlife. The broad well-defined path (with seats) skirts the lake with its mute swans, great-crested grebes, tufted ducks, moorhens and coots. At the western end, through a stone Gothic Arch is the Menagerie Garden, an area established on the site of a medieval quarry in the late 1750s. At its centre is the Menagerie House thought to have been designed by Paine but with wings added by Adam about 1776. It has a central portion called the Gothick Room with decorative plasterwork executed by

Joseph Rose the Elder. It was originally occupied by the menagerie keeper and his wife and later used as a gardener's cottage. A plan of 1758 shows that the Menagerie Garden was originally set out with a series of enclosures, which were probably aviaries. Some late eighteenth century accounts record poultry including turkeys, geese, ducks and drakes, being cared for by the keepers for twelve shillings a week.[7] The Menagerie House may be fully restored as an interpretation centre or exhibition space. At the back of the house, hidden amongst the undergrowth, is an ice-house (not accessible to the public). Also in this area is a pit for fighting cocks, constructed in 1783, to Francis Labron's design, where money changed hands and no doubt fortunes were lost! In the nineteenth century this area was laid out with formal flower-beds, decorated with urns and statues, a few of which remain. A statue of Venus is in National Trust storage at present but may be re-instated in this area. Evergreen shrubs and trees in the Menagerie *Rhododendron* Garden include rhododendron, yew, holly, Scots pine, bamboo, larch, Cedar of Lebanon and holm oak. Broad-leaved varieties growing here are cut-leaved beech, tulip tree, sycamore, turkey oak and sessile oak.

Another area worth visiting is the Stable block with a Rose Garden established in the 1920s to the south of it. The Stable block, commenced in the 1770s, had alterations and additions in the 1820s and 1870s including the construction of the stable's cupola to the original design of Robert Adam, which is a major visual element in the landscape.[8] The Rose Garden is bounded on the west by one of the walls of the eighteenth century kitchen garden (not open to the public). The current restoration programme is very exciting and will bring this park landscape back to its former splendour by opening up vistas, creating new walks within the park and repairing important historical structures. The programme is due for completion in 2007.

The Menagerie House.

The Italianate garden at Renishaw Hall.

RENISHAW HALL GARDENS AND PARK

Location: Two miles from Jct 30 of the M1 between Renishaw and Eckington approached from the A6135.

Ownership: Sir Reresby and Lady Sitwell.

Opening times & charges: Open from the beginning of April – end of September on Thursdays, Fridays, Saturdays, Sundays and Bank Holidays. 10.30am-4.30pm. Admission £3.50 adults and £2.50 concessions. Visit the website for further details and events at www.sitwell.co.uk or telephone 01246 432310.

Facilities: Car park; toilets. Georgian stable block which houses the Sitwell Museum, the John Piper Gallery (that hosts visiting exhibitions) and the Gallery café. Plant sales. Shop selling Renishaw Hall wine.

Special features: Grade II* formal Italian-style garden of about five acres with terraces, avenues, classical statues, fountains and pools. Also woodland and lakeside walks. Sculpture Park. National Collection of Yuccas in restored orangery. Splendid variety of trees, shrubs and flowering plants set within and around neatly-clipped yews and lawns. If you love plants you'll love Renishaw Hall gardens!

Sir George Sitwell's vision

Renishaw Hall has been the home of the Sitwell family since the early seventeenth century. The gardens we see today were largely designed and created by Sir George Sitwell between 1886 and 1936. Famous as a scholarly eccentric he and his wife Ida were parents of the literary trio, Edith, Osbert and Sacheverell. Sir George was the grandfather of the present owner.

Sir George Sitwell was passionate about Italian gardens and visited around 200 of them to research and develop his ideas on gardening. In 1909 he published a short book, *On the Making of Gardens*, subtitled – *a study of old Italian Gardens, of the Nature of Beauty and the Principles involved in Garden Design.* He stressed the importance of wonder and surprise, the value of contrast and the need for water. He believed the essential purpose of a garden was to provide a setting for the house.[1]

A Garden of Wonder and Surprise

On entering the gardens through the shrubbery on an April morning, the first enchanting view the visitor sees is an avenue of lime trees bordering crowds of daffodils. They stop by the recently discovered and gilded statue, *The Angel of Fame*. In this area, known as the Top Lawn, is an enormous oak tree planted in 1815 to commemorate the Battle of Waterloo. Also situated here is a Gothic Temple built in 1808 as a conservatory with glass dome and walls. It was later used as an aviary and is now a dogs' cemetery. Trees and shrubs on the Top Lawn include *Davidia involucrata*, the pocket-handkerchief tree, *Magnolia denudata* and various mop-head and lace-cap hydrangeas.[2] At the far end of the lime avenue is a brick wall with an orangery on its southern side now housing the National Collection of Yuccas. Over thirty species of Yuccas from the western United States are represented here.

Growing up the walls and planted in beds under the south front of Renishaw Hall are a number of delicate shrubs and climbers including magnolias, *Cytisus battanderii* (the pineapple tree), fig, wisteria, jasmine, honeysuckle, quince and hop. To the east of the house is a garden area planted in a blue, yellow and white colour scheme and beyond this a lawn with a magnificent fern-leaf beech, *Fagus sylvatica 'Asplenifolia'*. Directly in front of the house terrace is the Middle Lawn flanked by herbaceous borders, pink flowers on the west and blues and mauves on the east. At the southern end of the Middle Lawn are the statues of Diana and Neptune by the Italian, Calicari. On either side of this lawn are gardens of roses, each with a marble fountain.

The lime avenue with carpets of daffodils and the gilded statue, 'The Angel of Fame'.

Herbaceous border.

On descending the steps from the Middle Lawn to the next terrace the visitor enters the 'Swimming Pool' – not literally! The pool has a central plume of water, an innovation by Sir Reresby Sitwell, and is surrounded by over 200 roses. Steps between two more statues descend to the ha-ha and more floriferous borders. To the east of the pool area is a carp-filled ornamental pond with waxy water-lilies and a wrought iron footbridge. Another recently created garden, known as the Stone Tank Garden, for obvious reasons, lies to the east of the yew hedges. In summer the stone tank is planted with papyrus collected from the Nile by the Sitwells. The border has the giant *Gunnera manicata*, rogerosias, arum lilies, alliums and bamboos.[3]

Water lilies.

The Woods and Lakes

For those with energy left a walk in the woodlands and around the lakes is most rewarding. The Wilderness, or Broxhill Wood, is to the east of the main garden area. Take the route between the statues of Warrior and Amazon and proceed down the holly-hedged path towards a clearing called the New Woodland Garden. An alternative route takes the visitor down a camellia avenue planted in 1985. In May the woodlands are carpeted with bluebells.

The two main lakes at Renishaw were excavated in 1892 using unemployed fishermen from Scarborough where Sir George was the M.P. The third lake was formed in 2000. Near the middle lake is the old sawmill, a Victorian building, originally a power station used to drive water from the lakes up to the hall. It has a fantastic red brick chimney. Near the upper lake is an arch that was once the gatehouse to the entrance when the drive to the hall led straight over the River Rother.

Hercules wrestling with a lion.

The Sculpture Trail or Lady Ida's Walk

This walk, largely within the walls of the old kitchen garden takes in spectacular views across the Rother Valley with trees planted in the late nineteenth century to screen the railway lines, an iron works and a colliery. This area is host to modern sculptures by artists keen to show their work in a garden setting. First installed in 2002 the trail features over twenty romantic and figurative works.

Reclining figure, 'Morning', by Vanessa Pooley.

The Renishaw Vineyard
The vineyard at Renishaw was the most northerly vineyard in the world when it was planted in 1972. Occasionally the head gardener leads guided tours around the 1,500 vines for enthusiasts. The most successful vine was the Seyval Blanc. This is now supplemented with Madeline Angevine and a variety of Phoenix. There are also vineries in the kitchen garden where grapes for the table have been grown since 1913. Renishaw wine can be purchased from the shop and sampled in the café!

ROTHERHAM'S URBAN PUBLIC PARKS

Rotherham's two central urban parks have an association with two of the leading figures in the town's history. Boston Castle Park was developed on land where the Earl of Effingham built his hunting lodge which he provocatively called Boston Castle to show his displeasure at the government's policies towards the North American colonists in 1773. Clifton Park was formerly the grounds of the residence of Joshua Walker, a leading industrialist. Two other formal parks, not discussed below, are Rosehill Victoria Park in Rawmarsh (for which a new masterplan was drawn up in September 2004) and Bradgate Park in Kimberworth.

BOSTON CASTLE AND PARK
Location: At the end of Boston Castle Grove, off Moorgate Road, Rotherham.
Ownership: Rotherham Metropolitan Borough Council.
Facilities: Limited parking in the grounds.
Special features: Boston Castle, attractive bedding, good viewpoint over the Rother and Don Valleys and beyond, exposed rock-face of Rotherham Red Sandstone, proximity to the ancient Canklow Wood.

From quarry hills to public park
Under the Rotherham Enclosure Award of 1761-64 an area of rough land, known as quarry hills, then on the south-western outskirts of Rotherham, was awarded to Thomas Howard, 3rd Earl of Effingham (1747-91). In 1773 he began to build a gothic folly to be used as a hunting lodge and rural retreat. At the end of that year the foundations for the building were being dug and stone and lime transported to the site. It appears that festivities in the form of a firework display were held to mark the occasion. 'Rockit sticks at 2d each' and 'a Board with Letters on for the fire Works' were purchased.[1] The builders were John and James Bagshaw and their records refer to 'two foot walls … stone and brick work … a passage, two little chambers, the best chamber, a cellar with a stone keeping table and the Little House.'[2]

This square, two-storey battlemented building, which still stands, was called Boston Castle to commemorate the Boston Tea Party, the occasion in Boston, Massachusetts, in 1773 when over 300 chests of tea were dumped into the harbour following a fiery debate about the controversial tea tax being levied by England. This triggered the American War of Independence and the Earl of Effingham resigned his commission rather than fight in the war, which he thought was unjust. Apparently the Earl never allowed tea ('that obnoxious beverage'[3]) to be drunk in

Boston Castle.

Boston Castle instead his guests 'were plenteously regaled with wine and punch.'[4]

A century later Boston Castle and over twenty acres of adjoining land became Rotherham's first public park. Situated some 300 feet above the main town it offers extensive views. Writing in the 1870s, John Guest described the 'spacious amphitheatre, framed on every side but one, by wood-crowned hills, dotted all over by elegant mansions, pierced by navigable rivers ... and filled by human habitation,'[5] although he conceded that fifty chimneys had also been erected! He enthused about the neighbouring Canklow Wood with 'its fine sea-like murmur of waving boughs, and spring-tide carpeting of hyacinthine beauty.'[6] The *Rotherham Advertiser* was no less fulsome in its praise saying that 'no more delightful site could have been selected' and that whoever could 'admire the picturesque charms of nature could find them in rich abundance in this neighbourhood.' The correspondent went on eloquently by stating that the views from Boson Castle could 'vie with the places which evoke the enthusiasm of tourists in other lands.'[7] Praise indeed!

The Opening Ceremony

Boston Park was opened on the centenary of the Declaration of Independence – 4 July 1876 – by Rotherham's Mayor and Mayoress. Originally known as Rotherham Park or The People's Park it was designed by Henry Albiston, the park-keeper/curator who lived in Boston Castle (now a Grade II listed building). Henry Albiston (1822 1908) was born in Dalton, Rotherham and, prior to taking on the task of creating Boston Park from a disused stone quarry, had designed gardens at Aldwarke Hall, Owston Park, Ferham House and Oakwood Hall.

The proposed nineteenth century plan shows meandering walkways, avenues of trees, shrubberies and flower beds, bowling and croquet greens and, on an adjoining field, gymnastic and cricket facilities. Gymnastic equipment at that time often consisted of horizontal and parallel bars, swings and a giant stride. There were also

The re-erected doorway from Rotherham's fifteenth century College of Jesus.

rustic seats in a 'Lovers' Dale'. The park is bounded on the east by the rock face of the old quarry into which a doorway from Rotherham's fifteenth century College of Jesus was re-erected.

Town shops and businesses were closed for the opening ceremony, on the afternoon of 4 July. The sun shone and most of Rotherham's population were in holiday mood – but not all. Many Moorgate residents were opposed to the formation of the park, on their doorstep, open to all. They expected an influx of 'roughs' but were reassured that disorder would 'be repressed with some severity, that improper language would ensure expulsion from the grounds … and that annoyance of every description would be promptly punished.'[8] Over one hundred dignitaries from the local area were invited to the opening ceremony. Following the band, they 'beat the bounds' – that is, they made a circuit of the main pathways. There then followed numerous speeches and toasts before the park was declared open and lunch taken in a spacious marquee on the bowling green. The menu was sumptuous and included gelatine veal, ornamental hams and tongues, ducklings, lobster salad, pigeon pies, custards, blancmanges, brandy cream, gooseberry pie, Bakewell tarts and lemon cheese cake. Champagne, claret, hock and sherry flowed freely.[9] Music was provided by the Rotherham Rifle Volunteer Band and the Royal Excelsior Handbell Ringers who 'performed in a very talented manner.'[10]

Noteworthy Features and Interest
Boston Castle and Park became noted for its carpet bedding, a speciality of Henry Albiston. Over 40,000 plants were laid out, including two varieties of lobelia named 'Boston Castle' and 'Rotherham Park'.[11] In a newspaper report about the gardens in 1905 it was stated that 'visitors from far countries have gazed upon [the gardens] with feelings of admiration and pleasure' and that 'there is not anything in the parks of London that can be said to surpass them in delicacy of arrangement [and] in artistic blending of colour and bloom…'[12] Small areas of the park still excel with their formal bedding designs.

Spring bedding.

During the Second World War Boston Castle was used by the fire service as a look-out station. The Albiston family continued to provide wonderful floral displays until the 1950s. Celebrations organised by Rotherham Civic Society to mark the centenary of the park and the bicentenary of Boston Castle in 1976 were lavish. There was a wild west show, archery demonstrations, a display of Morris dancing, hot-air balloon ascents and parachutist descents and, of course, music and fireworks.[13]

The park once boasted some interesting items now sadly vanished – a beautifully carved brass and bronzed sundial presented by Isaac Walker in 1890;[14] an ancient archstone of St Anne's Well in Rotherham presented by local solicitor, Thomas Wright Badger;[15] a stone plaque with the Sheffield and Rotherham coat-of-arms (arrows and cannons) from Westgate Station surmounted by a stone bust and a millstone from a Rotherham windmill. This latter feature now forms the base of the siting stone situated at the top of the hillside. The Bowling Club, formed in 1916, still uses the park but their stone pavilion has been replaced. The park's proximity to Canklow Wood is an extra bonus as walks can be taken in this extensive ancient woodland.

The Future
A community support group, the Friends of Boston Castle and Parklands, was formed in 2002 and attempts are currently being made to secure funding for security lighting, the renovation of Boston Castle itself and the park generally.

Tibetan cherry tree.

CLIFTON PARK

Location: Bordering the town centre between Doncaster Road and Clifton Lane.
Ownership: Rotherham Metropolitan Borough Council.
Facilities: Limited car parking, café, toilets, recently-built children's play area, children's paddling pool, amusement area, tennis and bowling greens.
Special features: Formal, well-stocked floral beds of traditional planting, good display of spring bulbs, specimen trees, over 50 acres of parkland, war memorials, Roman granary remains, recently-refurbished Clifton House Museum with café and toilets.

Gallow Tree or Clifton?

The area now occupied by Clifton House Museum and Park was once part of one of Rotherham's open fields, known in 1764, as Gallow Tree Field. The field took its name from the Gallow Tree or Gibbet which it bordered, the latter being placed in a strategic location to deter wrongdoers. It was this site, together with some adjoining land, that was purchased by Joshua Walker in the 1780s, for the building of his new home, park and pleasure grounds. It is recorded in a minute book of 1783 that 'Mr Joshua Walker nearly compleated his new house, stables, etc, at Clifton.'[1] This is thought to be the earliest record of the name Clifton – a pleasanter-sounding name than Gallow Tree! The Walker family were industrialists who had established the Walker Iron and Steel Company at Masbrough in 1749. Due

Crocus in Clifton Park.

to the increased prosperity of the partners, Joshua and Susannah required a suitably impressive abode and grounds. At the time the elevated site would have given uninterrupted views of the surrounding area and was well away from the main industrial developments in Rotherham. It is thought that John Carr, the York architect, designed Clifton House. John Platt was also employed for some internal features, his diary stating '15 Jun 1784 Begun laying Staircase and hall floors Derbyshire marble at Clifton Joshua Walker, Esq.'[2]

The estate covered nearly seventy acres and consisted of a house, stables, outbuildings, a dovecote, wells and an ice-house. A Tithe map of 1837-38 clearly shows two walled gardens (one with glasshouses), a fishpond, lodge, driveways and groups of trees in a parkland setting.[3]

When Joshua Walker died in 1815 the estate passed to his elder son, Henry Frederick Walker and when he died in 1860 the entire estate was put up for sale. By this time Rotherham had expanded and the Clifton estate was no longer isolated. When the reserve price was not reached the estate was divided up into nine smaller lots. The largest part including the house, outbuildings, gardens, fishpond and lodge was sold to William Owen, another local industrialist, in 1864. William Owen died in 1883 and his wife, Catherine, the following year. This time the estate was split into seventeen lots, almost half being offered for building. However much of the park remained unsold until Rotherham Corporation bought the house and fifty-four acres of parkland for £25,000 in 1891 'for the use of the townspeople in perpetuity' thus providing the local growing population with a much needed 'breathing space.'[4] A further £5,000 was spent on improvements and Clifton Park was opened on 25 June 1891 – and what an occasion!

The Official Opening
The park was officially opened by the Prince and Princess of Wales (later King Edward VII and Queen Alexandra) accompanied by the Princesses Maud and Victoria. The royal party stayed the previous night at Wentworth Woodhouse with the Earl and Countess Fitzwilliam who were also special guests at the ceremony. As the party left Wentworth Woodhouse 'the barometer was in doubtful mood'[5] but fortunately the sun shone later in the day. On reaching the Corporation boundary the party were 'met by a guard of the Yorkshire Dragoons, followed by the liveried out-riders and mounted police.'[6] It had been suggested that Rotherham was much too radical a town to give the royal party 'a right royal reception' but they did, the royal party being 'greeted with the most cordial manner possible.'[7]

Messrs Pain and Sons provided the decorations that lined the route of the royal party. There were

> Venetian masts along the route with emblazoned shields, trophies and flags on poles … covered with Turkey red twill and surmounted by gilt spear heads with banners suspended from the top of each. Some streets had festoons of streamers, others flags … and there was a triumphal arch at the bridge at the end of Effingham Street.[8]

Also present for the opening ceremony were Rotherham's Mayor and his wife (Alderman and Mrs Neill), Councillor W B Hirst (Chairman of the Parks Committee) and the Town Clerk, Mr H H Hickmott. This was the first occasion at which the Mayor wore his newly acquired robes of office, cocked hat and mayoral chain (made by local jeweller, John Mason), the purchase of which had 'met with opposition against extravagance and vulgar display.' The Mayor obviously made a great impression as 'driving ahead of the royal carriage he was loudly cheered' and on stepping from his carriage ten thousand children, on specially erected stands, thought that he was the Prince of Wales, and began to sing their well-rehearsed song, *God Bless the Prince of Wales* to 'considerable merriment'![9]

During the afternoon there were many festivities for the crowds to enjoy – 'bands, coconut shies, dancing and a parachute jump.'[10] The main attraction however was a balloon ascent by Captain Whelan of Huddersfield. The balloon was filled with gas from the town mains. At the beginning of the ascent there was a near calamity when a local councillor got his legs entangled with the ropes and was almost carried aloft hanging upside down by his legs! Fortunately he managed to free himself before the balloon 'sped on its journey skywards and was carried over the town towards Thorpe Hesley.'[11] The balloon later landed safely on the moors nine miles from Huddersfield. The evening festivities were in the form of a grand firework display which included a portrait of the Mayor and Mayoress, a naval battle and the Borough arms.

The *Rotherham Advertiser* described the new park as 'beautifully wooded with trees of a rare type and others of majestic appearance'. The article went on to explain how Henry Albiston, the curator of Boston Park, was to create a number of flower beds 'in elegant designs' on the lawns to the east of Clifton House (which became a museum in 1893). A grotto is also described 'intended to represent a miniature cave' in which 'stalactites' hung from the roof and where the interior was 'studded with coral, fossils, shells, petrifications and various other interesting geological specimens', while the exterior was 'adorned with other fossils.'[12]

Council Minutes over the next three years indicate the changing nature of the landscape. Fifty seats were installed in the park, the fruit and vegetables from the old kitchen garden were sold (for £103 8s 0d), the ha-ha was filled in to make it safe for

Park staff posing outside the grotto at Clifton Park.

Ornamental lake at Clifton Park in the 1920s.

visitors, hundreds of chestnut, lime and elm trees were planted especially along newly-created walkways and the tenants of Birdcage Lodge were given notice to leave! In 1892 a park ranger, Mr Roots, was installed in the lodge, the fishpond was made into a shallow lake with an island in it and a bandstand was erected – what commitment![13]

The Twentieth Century Park

The main entrance to Clifton Park at the corner of Clifton Lane and Doncaster Road was improved in about 1900 with the installation of massive pillars and cast iron gates. Unfortunately the gates were removed in the Second World War. The original cast iron bandstand was removed to Ferham Park in 1919 and a First World War tank then occupied the site until 1927. A new bandstand was erected in 1928 and was renovated in 1991 to mark the park's centenary.

The bandstand erected in 1928 and still used for concerts.

In 1920 the bases and shafts of columns from the granary of Templeborough Roman Fort were incorporated into the garden behind Clifton House after their removal from the site by Thomas May in 1916-17. These are still an interesting feature for examination with a new interpretation board alongside. Steps from this area lead to a small garden area with a sundial, made by Samuel Walker, in its centre. In November 1922 the cenotaph, designed by Lieutenant Colonel J E Knight, was unveiled with twelve bronze panels containing the names of the 1,304 Rotherham men who had lost their lives in the First World War. The memorial gardens around the cenotaph opened in 1948. Tennis courts were opened in 1923 on the site of the old kitchen garden to be followed a year later by putting and bowling greens (all well-maintained). The lake had ducks and wildfowl, an ornamental shelter and a drinking fountain near-by. It was popular for fishing and ice-skating on in cold winters. The lake was later thought be be insanitary and was replaced in 1939 by a children's paddling pool. This area of the park gradually developed as a children's play area with swings and roundabouts, a menagerie, donkey rides (the donkeys were retired in 1996), a miniature railway (closed in 1997) and a roller skating rink. It is still a popular spot for families with young children as there is an amusement area, adventure playground and the traditional swings. To the west of Clifton House is a rockery (which once had a series of tumbling watercourses and ponds). With almost 8,000 tons of stone quarried at Hooton Levitt, and thousands of interesting plants including maples and dwarf conifers, it must have been quite splendid once. In autumn the maples are still a treat.

During the Second World War Clifton Park was the venue for the Holidays at Home programme. Children could meet with 'Uncle Harry' (Harry Woodcock) and sing:

Sunshine Corner
Oh, it's jolly fine
It's for children
Under ninety-nine.
All are welcome
Seats are given free
Clifton's Sunshine Corner
Is the place for me.

Local residents also recall the Barage Balloon site near the sunken garden run by WAAFs.

For decades the park was also the location for the annual Whit Sing. Today the park continues to attract visitors and Rotherham residents to its open, landscaped spaces, to admire the drifts of spring flowering bulbs, the summer bedding and the autumn colours and to special events such as the annual Rotherham Show. The play facilities and the sports provision are well-maintained. Steps are currently being taken to secure additional funding for this important heritage park. A visit to the recently-refurbished museum can also be recommended.

SHEFFIELD BOTANICAL GARDENS
Location: Situated less than one mile from Sheffield city centre. Entrances are from Thompson Road via Ecclesall Road (A625), on Clarkehouse Road and on Brocco Bank.

Opening times and charges: In the winter months 8am-4pm weekdays and 10am-4pm weekends. During the summer months 8am-dusk weekdays and 10am-dusk weekends. Free admission.

Facilities: Tearoom and restaurant in the former Curator's House, toilets.

Special Features: Recently restored Grade II* glasshouses; nineteen acres of refurbished gardens with two Grade II listed lodges and a bear pit. Themed gardens. Wonderful variety of trees from around the world. National collections of *Weigela* and *Diervilla*. Visit the website for details of events at www.sbg.org.uk.

To promote healthy recreation and self education

In June 1833 the Sheffield Botanical and Horticultural Society was formed to develop a botanical garden. After a few months £7,500 had been raised in shares of £20 each and by the following year eighteen acres of south-facing fertile farmland had been purchased from Joseph Wilson, snuff maker of Sharrow. A national competition was held to obtain a design for the gardens, glass pavilions, entrance and lodges with Joseph Paxton (of Chatsworth and Crystal Palace fame) as one of the judges. Robert Marnock, gardener at Bretton Hall, won first prize and Benjamin Broomhead Taylor, a Sheffield architect, was awarded second prize.[1] In May 1834 the Society appointed Robert Marnock to act as their first curator at a salary of £100 per annum. He laid out the gardens in the then highly fashionable 'gardenesque' style, where each plant was displayed to perfection in scattered plantings. Designs of botanical gardens tended to be functional rather than aesthetic providing opportunities for self education in botany and horticulture.

The recently restored pavilions in Sheffield Botanical Gardens.

The design for the glass pavilions, often referred to as Paxton's Pavilions, is thought to be a result of collaboration between Marnock, Taylor, Paxton and John C Loudon.[2] The resulting structure, almost 100 metres long, in five distinct sections, incorporates three very early examples of curvilinear glass pavilions. The three lofty quadrangular glazed domes had wrought-iron ribs with ornamental castings and Corinthian stone pillars. These were joined by glass walkways in the 'ridge and furrow' style of Paxton's glasshouse at Chatsworth. Originally the central pavilion was a tropical palm house with the two smaller pavilions, at either end, housing temperate plants.

The grand entrance from Clarkhouse Road, designed by Taylor, is through an elegant lodge-gateway in the Ionic style of architecture. Nearby a house was built for the curator to the same high standard. The lower lodge was built in the style of a Swiss cottage and is approached from Thompson Road. From the front of the central conservatory a grand promenade path, about 180 metres long, descended to a fountain (recently re-instated). A contemporary report described the tasteful grounds

> *laid out in artificial rockwork and water, traversed by winding paths and romantic dells, and having … small ponds, a rustic bridge, subterraneous archways, grottos, a hermitage, aviaries … bear pit … and an ancient wood.*

It went on to describe the specimens of both British plants and exotics, the

> *spacious walks and grass-plots, for the assemblage of the numerous visitors who throng hither on public promenade days, when commodious tents are erected, and the enhancing scene is enlivened by music.*[3]

The Grand Opening

The gardens were opened to the general public on 29 and 30 June and 4 and 5 July 1836 – by ticket only! Admission was two shillings for adults and one shilling for children under 14 on the first two days and half the price on the next two days.[4] The newspaper advertisement promised that the committee would 'spare no Expense in making the Fete on the opening of the Extensive Gardens and Pleasure Grounds most attractive'; and although the Grounds were not completely finished their already 'advanced state of beauty, together with the variety of architectural magnificence in the surrounding picturesque Scenery' could not 'fail to strike the Visitor with delight.' Two bands were to 'enliven the gaity of the days' and refreshments 'of the very best kind' were to be provided 'at moderate charges.' Apparently more than 12,000 people visited on the opening days. No doubt, 'anybody who was anybody' would have been there!

Mixed Fortunes

In 1840 Robert Marnock left Sheffield to become curator of the Royal Botanic Society's garden at Regent's Park. After a financial crisis in 1844 the gardens thrived under the care of two curators, first John Law and then John Ewing. John Law's plant lists are collectors' items. In 1849 Law listed over seventy species and varieties of camellias and over sixty fuchsias and pelargoniums. In the hot-house he boasted that '156 species including bananas, plantain, gigantic dracaena, yucca, fig and olive trees and eighty-three species of orchid were to be found in the Orchid House'.[5] One of the greatest horticultural achievements of the Victorian period was the cultivation of the *Victoria Regia* water-lily. The *Sheffield Telegraph* reported that 'the curator

Dee Jones with macaws from the aviary, 1968.

placed a chair on one of the leaves and sat on it. Some of the gardeners also sat upon it. At one time the weight upon the leaf was upwards of 160 lbs. The largest leaf measured 7ft 10½ inches in diameter.'[6] There are other local records describing this 'most gorgeously beautiful of all water lilies with its enormous leaves and gigantic flowers.'[7]

Entertainments were frequently held in the gardens. Promenade concerts were very popular at which 'ladies dressed in their best, chatted and flirted to the music of the band.' Apparently a number of Sheffield marriages were hatched at the 'Prom'.[8] Amusements were also laid on including on one occasion Blondin, the tight-rope walker. In the mid 1850s even the bear pit had bears! Advertisements in the *Sheffield and Rotherham Independent* for 8 August 1892 tell of magnificent illuminations and fireworks (by C T Brock and Co.) with 10,000 coloured lamps and lanterns in the Botanical Gardens. The firework display was to depict 'The Durbar at Delhi, at the Proclamation of the Empress of India, showing the Jumna Musjid amid Waving Palms and Parading Elephants.' The Scots Guards Band and the Pipers of the Scots Guards were to provide 'reels, strathspeys and sword dances' – all for one shilling!

Between 1836 and 1898 entry into the Botanical Gardens was limited to shareholders and annual subscribers, except for special fetes and galas when entry was still sufficiently expensive to exclude the majority of Sheffield's population. Metal tokens were used to gain access to the gardens.There were real problems in August 1897 when the curator was dismissed, nearly all the gardeners discharged and all the plants in the houses sold. The gardens were in debt – but only by £22! It was suggested that some shareholders would have liked to see the gardens sold, possibly for building purposes. The Town Trust came to the rescue, took over the management and instituted free entry for all. There was, however, still that element of social control. Uniformed commissionaires supervised the entrances to make sure that 'no person of notoriously bad character' could enter the gardens (we wonder how they were recognised) 'nor any person in a state of intoxication, or suffering from any contagious infection or loathsome disease, or so dirty in clothes or person as to be an annoyance to the public.'[9]

For the first half of the twentieth century the Town Trust managed the gardens. During the Second World War the pavilions were badly damaged by German bombing in Sheffield. In 1951 Sheffield Corporation took over the management of the gardens and repaired the three glass pavilions (the two glass walkways had already been lost) in 1958. In the 1960s and 1970s the central pavilion housed an aviary and the east pavilion an aquarium. The gardens were developed as a centre for horticultural education, notably under the curatorship of Don Williams (1968-89). For the last two decades of the twentieth century financial restrictions resulted in neglect. The pavilions were closed to the public from the late 1980s having become dilapidated.

Repair, Restoration and Regeneration

The Friends of the Botanical Gardens was formed in 1984 to act as a support group. In 1996 a partnership between the Friends, the Town Trust (owners), Sheffield City Council (managers) and the University of Sheffield made a bid to the Heritage Lottery Fund for complete restoration of the entire gardens – buildings and plantings. An award of just over £5 million was announced in May 1997. This required matched funding of around £1.25 million – an enormous task! But what a transformation! The Curator's House is now an excellent tearoom and restaurant, the gatehouse is renovated and the pavilions wonderfully restored to their former splendour and planted imaginatively with such exotics as Voodoo Lily, Kangaroo Paw and White Lobster Claw! The east pavilion has plants from South-

Tree ferns in the pavilions.

Two pieces of public art on the Riddle Trail.

east Asia such as grapefruit, banana and cloves. The central glasshouse has a fountain and an array of Australian plants including acacias, Banksias and bottlebrushes. The west pavilion houses plants from South Africa. The east 'ridge and furrow' walkway has Asian and Himalayan collections including camellias and rhododendrons. New Zealand plants are displayed in the west 'ridge and furrow' house with attractive tree ferns. This area also shows the flora of South America – the climber *Lapageria rosea,* passion flowers and angels' trumpets. These restored pavilions were officially opened by Prince Charles in September 2003.

Work has continued in the rest of the gardens with tree surveys being undertaken resulting in thinning and new plantings. The garden areas are now 'themed.' One area has a taste of the North American prairies with swathes of wild prairie grasses. This contrasts with an 'evolution' garden displaying ancient Giant Redwood and Ginkgo trees and the 300 million years old fossilised tree stump. There is a Four Seasons garden with a sensory theme, an Asian garden showing trees and shrubs from China and the Himalayas and a Mediterranean garden with sun-loving plants. The bear pit even has a grizzly bear (thankfully made of metal). The rose garden has been completely overhauled and restored to its original design with plantings of over 200 varieties of traditional and modern roses. The bronze statue of Pan, Spirit of the Woods, presented to the garden in 1934 under the terms of the will of Sir Charles Clifford, has been renovated and forms a centrepiece to the rose garden.

A novel idea for children, young and old, is the Riddle Trail which consists of eight new pieces of public art, each incorporating a riddle written by Sheffield children's author Berlie Doherty. Riddles in the trail include a hand-carved oak bench (with a frog, squirrel, moth and mouse), a mosaic plaque incorporating a protea flower, an acorn in stone and a riddle within dinosaur footprints cast in brass.

These gardens are once again gardens to be proud of. They are free to all and can still promote healthy recreation and self education.

SHEFFIELD'S URBAN PUBLIC PARKS

Sheffield's urban parks – of which there are over a dozen – encircle the city like pearls on a necklace, as one writer described them. Eight are discussed below. They vary in age from the very early Victorian period (Norfolk Park, 1841) to the 1950s (Whirlow Brook Park). A number of parks incorporate or lead to semi-natural, informal countryside. Some important and historic parks (Abbeyfield, High Hazels, Glen Howe and Graves) have had to be excluded for lack of space.

The city centre green space that is a must for the visitor features the Peace Gardens and the Winter Garden. The Peace Gardens were developed on the site of St Paul's church which was demolished in 1938. The area has recently been redesigned with magnificent new stonework and balustrades, water channels, a grid of multi-jet fountains, grassy banks and imaginative planting. The Winter Garden, Sheffield's new temperate glasshouse, was opened in December 2002 with a children's candlelight procession and fireworks. Formed of ten pairs of high parabolic wooden arches, reaching up to twenty-two metres, this award-winning structure houses over 150 species of plants mainly from the Southern Hemisphere. Many of these will bloom in winter. Underfloor heating protects the plants from the frost. It is open 8am-6pm every day. Visit the website on www.sheffield.gov.uk.

The Peace Gardens with the Winter Garden in the background. Inset: *Winter Garden interior.*

FIRTH PARK

Location: 2¹/₂ miles north-east of Sheffield City centre, bisected by Firth Park Road (B6086).

Facilities: Almost 40 acres incorporating an ancient woodland. Bowling green, multi-sports area, children's playground (opened in April 2004), with a 75-place *First Start* nursery, café, toilets, ranger base, exhibition/meeting rooms completed in 2004. Community rooms at the nineteenth century Clock Tower building. Website: www.firthpark.org.uk.

The Opening Ceremony

Firth Park was Sheffield's first publicly-owned park. It was donated by public benefactor Mark Firth 'to his Native Town'[1] in 1875. Mark Firth was the eldest son of Thomas Firth of the famous steel and gun forging firm of Sheffield. Mark inherited the business which developed with great success. In 1840 he purchased the late eighteenth century Page Hall and its extensive grounds in what was then a rural location. It is part of that estate that forms Firth Park.

The opening ceremony took place on 16 August 1875 when Mark Firth was Mayor of Sheffield. It was opened by Edward, Prince of Wales, the future King Edward VII, and his wife, Princess Alexandra. And what an occasion! Preparations had taken months and Sheffield was 'dressed and decorated out of all recognition.'[2] The royal couple were met at the Victoria Railway Station, which had been transformed into a huge conservatory, by the Mayor and Mayoress, the Master Cutler, the Dukes of Norfolk and Rutland, the Archbishop of York, Earl Fitzwilliam and other distinguished guests. After a royal salute had been fired, the procession, consisting of forty carriages, was led by the band of the 7th Hussars and a squadron of the West Yorkshire Yeomanry Cavalry. The route taken, almost eight miles in length, was lined by cheering 'crowds of orderly and eager spectators anxious to cheer the Prince and Princess as soon as they should appear.'[3] The town (it was not then a city) was adorned in bunting and every yard of the route had its banner, escutcheon, Venetian mast or floral decoration to add splendour to the scene. One reporter said that

The opening ceremony at Firth Park, 16 August 1875. The Graphic, 21 August 1875

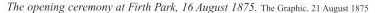

'Triumphal arches were almost as plentiful as blackberries.'[4] One such arch was a facsimile in canvas and wood of old Sheffield castle, garrisoned by a number of small boys in warlike attire.

When the royal party arrived at the entrance to the park a salute was fired by a military battery and the Prince and Princess took their seats in a 'grand pavilion' crowned by 'a large Turkish minaret'. Directly opposite the pavilion were 15,000 Sunday School scholars who sang the National Anthem accompanied by military bands. The Archbishop of York said a prayer, Mark Firth handed over to the Prince the deeds of the park, in which he dedicated it 'for ever to the public use and enjoyment of the people'. The Prince in his turn presented them to the Town Clerk declaring the park to be opened. The declaration was received with a fanfare of trumpets and another salvo of artillery and renewed cheering from the crowds. Their Royal Highnesses then went to Mark Firth's villa, Oakbrook, in Ranmoor. The public stayed in their thousands to enjoy the rest of that summer afternoon and evening in their new park.

Bye-laws for Firth Park

Sheffield Council met in August 1876 and issued a set of twenty bye-laws for the newly established Firth Park. They reflect Victorian attitudes and values. Opening times were stipulated, varying according to the season, but never on Sunday mornings when it was expected that residents should be at church or chapel. Officials were keen to preserve the appearance of the park and ordered that 'no person … shall carelessly, negligently, or improperly' remove or spoil any 'fence, seat, barrier, gate, or notice board.' No-one could 'cut, fell, burn or break' any tree, shrub or plant nor could they 'deposit or leave … any stone, sand, refuse, rubbish, manure, or dead animal.' It was forbidden to shake or beat a carpet or rug in the park or use the pleasure grounds for drying or bleaching. No person was allowed to 'break in or exercise any horse, ass, or mule on, over, or across' the park. It was prohibited to graze or feed 'any cattle, sheep, swine, horse, ass, mule, turkey, goose, duck, fowl, or other animal.' Wildlife was protected by rules to prevent anyone from catching birds or taking their eggs. Other bye-laws stipulated that only those authorised by the Council could sell refreshments in the park and, of course, no-one could sell 'intoxicating liquors.' The playing of games and musical instruments was forbidden on Sundays. A penalty of £5 was issued for each offence!

Early History

For almost the next 100 years every part of the 36-acre park flourished and was heavily used. The park is made up of a long spur of land flanked by two valleys each containing a small stream. The western stream was once dammed forming two small linear lakes with weirs. The promontory had paths for 'promenading' and areas for formal (cricket and football) and informal games. The two valleys were (and remain) wooded. Brushes Wood, in the east, is an ancient oak wood mentioned in 1637 as a spring (coppice) wood. In 1909 Hinde Common Wood, to the south of Brushes Wood, was purchased and added to the park.

The main entrance to the park was at the Clock Tower and this is where Firth Park Road stopped in 1875. At the northern end of the park the North Lodge was built

Looking towards the drinking fountain and ornamental sheet of water with the Clock Tower in the background.

near the Bell House farm complex. Both buildings were designed by local architects Flockton & Abbot. The Clock Tower was the focal point of the park in its early days. It incorporated the park keeper's house, rooms for refreshment, and a verandah where visitors could shelter in inclement weather. Immediately to the north was an ornamental sheet of water which towards the end of the nineteenth century had not only about a dozen ducks of various breeds but also a pair of swans and a parading peacock.

Park Attractions in the Past

Beside the northern end of the pond was a striking drinks fountain in a stone basin enclosed within an iron fence. In the centre, supporting the fountain, were three 'celestial mermaids', half-angel and half-fish. Attached to the fountain was a copper-faced drinking cup.[5] Another important and very-well used part of the park was the 'gymnasium', a physical education area, with its swings, horizontal and parallel bars, and a 'giant stride', a pole from which hung ropes and chains, which turned round the pole and on which children hung and made great leaps as it revolved. Such was the popularity of the park that it was estimated that at the end of the 1800s as many as 1,000 people

'Old Man of the Wood' carving by Jason Thomson in Brushes Wood.

103

A concert in the old bandstand at Firth Park.

visited the park every day in spring and summer and that on Good Friday the number of visitors might be as great as 30,000!

One of the great occasions in the past which continued until within living memory was the annual Whit Sing at which Sunday School scholars and their friends and families met in huge numbers to parade with their chapel banners and to sing to the accompaniment of a band around the bandstand. Musical concerts were frequently held around the bandstand – some on summer evenings when the bandstand was lit by hundreds of lamps.

One organisation that has stood the test of time is Firth Park Bowling Club, one of the founder members of Sheffield & District Crown Green Bowling Association. In 1949 a new entrance layout to Firth Park was approved near the present roundabout. The 1950s saw a rose garden established near the North Lodge and in

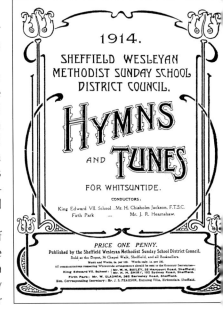

Hymn sheet cover for a Whitsuntide sing, 19.

the 1960s the duck pond was often used for model ship regattas. In the 1970s a children's playground was constructed near Hucklow Road – then came the years of decline.

The Rebirth of Firth
Now things are improving. Sheffield was a successful applicant in the Government's *Neighbourhood Nurseries Initiative*. The application was for the replacement of the Shiregreen Young Children's Centre with an innovative new space in Firth Park. The new nursery, at the top of the park, costing £1.8m, was completed in 2004 with 75 places for pre-school children as well as office space, a café, a meeting room, exhibition space, public toilets and a ranger base.

A new £100,000 playground was opened in April 2004. Most exciting of all, a Masterplan has been devised for regeneration of the park. Funding from the Heritage Lottery Fund is now being sought to implement this Masterplan. The main priorities of the plan in the short and medium term are for the multi-sports area to be upgraded, to create a youth space for skateboarding, BMX and roller blading, to improve the bowling facilities and develop a formal garden with quiet sitting areas. It is hoped that the former lake can be developed as an informal wetland area and that a new children's play area can be built at the Cammell Road end of the park.

HILLSBOROUGH PARK
Location: 2½ miles north-west of the city centre between Penistone Road (A61) and Middlewood Road (B6079).
Facilities: Library, car parks, tennis courts, bowling greens and pavilion, athletic sports arena, children's playground, lake for fishing.
Special features: Large eighteenth century Grade II listed classical house (now the library); coach house and stables; section of ha-ha to the south of the house; two lodges; ornamental lake, tree-lined avenues, walled garden redeveloped by the Hillsborough Community Development Trust who also occupy the old stable block.

History of the Site
The present park was originally the private grounds of Hillsborough House, built in 1779 in the Adam-style of architecture for Thomas Steade. It was named in honour of Lord Downshire who lived at Hillsborough Castle in County Down and it was Hillsborough House that gave this district of Sheffield its name.[1] The grounds were laid out in the late eighteenth century in the tradition of English landscape parks with groups of trees in open parkland, avenues of trees (predominantly lime), a lake and walled kitchen garden. In the mid-nineteenth century the house was occupied by John Rodgers (of Joseph Rodgers & Sons, famous cutlery manufacturers) and he changed the name to Hillsborough Hall. By 1865 it was in the possession of James Willis Dixon, a silver plater of Cornish Place, and then inherited by his son, James Willis Dixon in 1883. Sheffield Corporation bought Hillsborough Park (excluding the hall and about fifteen acres around it) for £15,000 at auction in 1890 from the trustees of the late James Willis Dixon.

The park was opened on 8 August 1892 after various improvements had been carried out by the Corporation to provide facilities for the public. The lake was enlarged to about three acres of water with tree-clad islands and made suitable for boating. New boundary walls and fences were erected and public conveniences were built. Along the Penistone

The Adam-style Hillsborough Hall (now Hillsborough Library) with the ha-ha in the foreground.

The now demolished bandstand in Hillsborough Park.

Road boundary the walls were built to a height of 2$\frac{1}{2}$ feet and topped with iron railings so that travellers, either on foot or in a vehicle, could view the park. New walks were created and sports facilities were provided.[2] In 1903 the hall was purchased and opened as a branch library with a reading room, lending room and a small picture gallery. Near the library there was once a splendid bandstand, a focal point for open-air concerts and Whit Sings. During the Second World War much of the park was given over to wartime use as allotments for food production under the 'Dig for Victory' campaign.

The Park Today

Hillsborough Park plays host to *Mayfest*, an extravaganza of entertainment over the Spring Bank holiday. The lake ceased to be used for boating around 1960 but has a few ducks and moorhens and is used for fishing. The lodges survive. The eighteenth century lodge on Penistone Road is being restored by Yorkshire Water following major improvement works in the area and will provide community and ranger facilities. The one on Middlewood Road, built in the 1840s when the road was turned into a turnpike, is home to a park-keeper and surrounded by formal bedding. Funding is currently being sought to restore the Coach House as a café and performance space.

The Walled Garden

Dating back to the late eighteenth century, the red brick heated walls once enclosed the kitchen garden of Hillsborough House. When the ownership passed to Sheffield Corporation in 1903 this area became a nursery and training centre for the Council's horticulturalists. In 1983 the site was abandoned and became derelict and there were proposals to turn the site into a car park. Several local interest groups formed a working partnership and put forward an alternative plan – the redevelopment of the garden. Work commenced in July 1991 with just £500 and voluntary help from

The Memorial Garden within the former walled kitchen garden of Hillsborough Hall.

schools, colleges, the probation service and local residents. The garden was opened by the Duke of Kent on 15 April 1993, the anniversary of the Hillsborough Stadium Disaster of 1989 in which 96 supporters lost their lives. The disaster has been permanently commemorated in the creation of a Memorial Garden within the walled garden alongside rose beds containing the specially commissioned bright red rose, 'Liverpool Remembers'. The 'Shankly Gates' stand at the garden's main entrance.

The walled garden has a formal area of planting with wide pathways suitable for wheelchair users, a pergola covered in laburnum, wisteria and clematis, a sensory garden, shrubbery and numerous seats. In a greenhouse, staffed by volunteers and trainees, a wide range of plants are grown. Alongside the walled garden is a wildlife garden. This area is a delightful, tranquil retreat away from the busy streets of Hillsborough.

THE LIMB VALLEY – WHINFELL QUARRY GARDENS AND WHIRLOW BROOK PARK
Location: Four miles south-west of Sheffield city centre accessed from Ecclesall Road South (A625).
Facilities: Car park, toilets and refreshments at Whirlow Brook Park.
Special features: Ornamental quarry garden planted in 1898 (Whinfell Quarry Garden); park created from a woodland and water garden of the 1920s (Whirlow Brook Park) and a wooded and moorland river valley.

Whinfell Quarry Gardens
This ornamental quarry garden was created in 1898 as part of the extensive grounds of Whinfell House. Samuel Doncaster, a notable local industrialist, had the house built and he commissioned the firm of James Backhouse and Son from York Nurseries to supply the plants for the new garden which consisted of a terraced area with the quarry garden below.[1] The derelict flagstone quarry provided an ideal microclimate for the growing of rare and exotic plants. The quarry has steep winding paths and steps, a few rock pools and some rare plants, shrubs and trees including bamboo, giant gunnera, redwoods, weeping beech, cedars, maples, flowering cherries, rhododendrons and conifers.

Giant gunnera in Whinfell Quarry Gardens.

The wooded Limb valley.

In 1912 Clarence Elliott, a nationally acclaimed British horticulturalist, plant-hunter and nurseryman, was commissioned to design the smaller quarry as a limestone rock garden.[2] Here many alpines, shrubs, deciduous trees and conifers were planted. In 1933 Frederick Neill purchased the house from Samuel Doncaster. In the 1960s there were major renovations to the gardens, including extensive replanting. In 1968 the gardens were presented to the city by James Neill Holdings Ltd as a memorial to Sir Frederick Neill. In 1971 Whinfell House was destroyed by fire and demolished. Flats now occupy the site of the house. Over recent years the gardens have suffered through lack of maintenance. It is a forgotten garden and deserves greater recognition – and funding.

Whirlow Brook Park and the Limb Valley beyond
Just to the west of Whinfell Quarry Gardens is the Limb valley with Whirlow Brook Park at its southern end. From Ecclesall Road South a path takes the visitor past a lake, once the upper dam of Whirlow Wheel known to have been in existence in 1586 and still in use in the 1920s. In 1665 it was a corn mill. By 1827 it was a saw grinding mill and was later used for scythe making. The path then leads to Whirlow Brook Park purchased by the Town Trustees and the J G Graves Charitable Trust in 1946 and presented to the city. It was opened to the public in June 1951. Whirlow Brook House was built in 1906 by Mr and Mrs Percy Fawcett. Mr Fawcett's sister and husband, Mr and Mrs Walter Benton Jones moved into the house in 1920 and invited the Royal Horticultural Society to advise on planting and planning the grounds during the late 1920s.[3] The gardens that were created, so typical of the time, remain just about intact. There is a rock garden constructed of millstone grit, two pools and a lower lake. The house is now a restaurant. As with many parks insufficient funding has resulted in lack of maintenance in the gardens and work is needed before the character is lost.

Continuing up the valley the path leads through mixed woodlands and eventually into much more open ground with young birch and hawthorn and wet pasture land and heath. The stream is boulder strewn and most attractive. At the top of the valley is the Round House, once a toll house built in 1795 on the Sheffield to Hathersage road.

MEERSBROOK PARK

Location: Two miles south of the city centre, accessed from Brook Road or Norton Lees Lane.

Facilities: Almost 45 acres with bowling greens, multi-sport hard surfaced courts; small children's playground.

Special features: Old walled kitchen garden run by the Meersbrook Park Users' Trust and Heeley City Farm (open to the public during normal working hours and for special events); Bishops' House Museum (telephone 0114 2782600 for opening times); commanding views of the city.

'Something better than mere promenades'

Meersbrook Hall, built in the mid-1700s was once the residence of Benjamin Roebuck, a prosperous merchant. The estate then passed to the Shore family, then the family of William Pashley Milner and eventually to a syndicate of London stockbrokers, the Lands Allotment Co Ltd.[1] Thirty-seven acres were purchased by Sheffield Corporation in 1886 to prevent the land being acquired for housing and to provide 'something better than mere promenades like Weston Park and the Botanical Gardens.'[2] There were further additions of land in 1928 and 1964.

On April 1890 Meersbrook Hall was opened as the Ruskin Museum in the new Meersbrook Park, a splendid attraction for residents and visitors alike. The hall now houses Sheffield Council's Parks, Woodlands and Countryside Department and some of the wonderful array of paintings, prints, murals and drawings brought together by John Ruskin are in part of the Millennium Galleries in central Sheffield. In its early days Meersbrook Park offered the opportunity to promenade along 'The Avenue',

The rustic bridge (now gone) over The Glen in Meersbrook Park.

A big sing at Whitsuntide.

around an ornamental rose garden and through a rockery with a cascade walk (crossed by a rustic bridge) known as 'The Glen'. This has mostly been lost. Similarly, the drinking fountain – of stone and Aberdeen granite – unveiled in August 1891 in memory of William Westran, one of the founders of the British Order of Oddfellows, no longer functions and is in a dilapidated state. The bandstand, once situated near the fountain, has also gone. Local bands gave concerts twice a day on some occasions and, of course, the bandstand was the focus for annual Whit sings.

In the 1890s one of the glories of Meersbrook Park was its rookery of about fifty nests. It was reported that one rook which fell from its nest was brought up by hand and became a perfectly tame pet and was 'on excellent terms with the curator's big St Bernard dog'.[3] The kitchen garden adjoining Meersbrook Hall was purchased by the Corporation and contained greenhouses and fruit trees. It now provides training and volunteering opportunities for a wide range of people in the community. Vocational courses in ornamental and amenity horticulture are conducted by Heeley City Farm (on 0114 2580482) in this garden.

The Park Today
Because of its steep nature, grassy banks and mature trees Meersbrook Park remains an attraction. From the top of the park there are wonderful panoramic views of the city. A visit to Bishops' House Museum (situated on Norton Lees Lane) at the highest point of the park is a must. The building is probably the best example of a timber-framed house surviving in Sheffield. It was the home of a yeoman farmer/scythe-maker, built about 1500. It has some wonderful timber work which can be examined at close quarters. Alterations and additions made between 1500 and 1700 reflect the rising prosperity of the owners and new standards of comfort. It was opened as a museum in 1976 and has free admission.

NORFOLK PARK

Location: Situated one mile south of the city centre with entrances on Guildford Avenue, Granville Road and Norfolk Park Road.

Facilities: A recently-built 'Centre in the Park' community building (with crèche, a café, meeting rooms, toilets), new children's playgrounds, bowling green and pavilion, tennis courts and football pitches. For information about the park call the Centre in the Park on 0114 2860400 or visit the Friends of Norfolk Heritage Park website at www.norfolk-park.com.

Special Features: 70 acres of park containing three restored Victorian park lodges, splendid views of the city, avenues of lime and turkey oak, area of ancient woodland with stream. Grade II listed.

A gatepost at Norfolk Park.

From Deer Park to Designed Park

During the medieval period, the land now occupied by Norfolk Park formed part of Sheffield Park, a deer park of almost 2,500 acres. During the sixteenth century Sheffield Park was owned by the Earls of Shrewsbury and it was in the midst of this park that Manor Lodge was built as a hunting and banqueting hall away from the town centre. The 6th Earl of Shrewsbury was the gaoler of Mary, Queen of Scots, between 1570 and 1584 and she stayed at the Manor Lodge when Sheffield Castle was being cleaned (and searched!). As well as containing 1,000 fallow deer Sheffield Park, as mentioned earlier, was famous for its enormous old pollarded trees of massive girth. In the mid-seventeenth century the park passed through marriage to the Howard family, the Dukes of Norfolk. By the early eighteenth century much of the park had been divided into farms and some parts were mined for ironstone.

In 1841 the Duke of Norfolk began a design for a park to provide much needed recreational space for the rapidly growing town. The seventy acre Norfolk Park opened in 1848 with free access for the general public – one of the first public parks in Britain. The layout was simple with open spaces for cricket and football, a shady peripheral walk or ride with regularly placed seats and avenues of lime trees and turkey oaks. In 1851 the stone screen and gates together with both lodges were built at Norfolk Park Road and Guildford Avenue. This latter lodge now houses the Norfolk Park 'Out of School Project' known as *The Maypole*. The Granville Road screen and entrance gates were erected in 1876.

'Strike Loud Notes of Triumph'

On 21 May 1897, Queen Victoria visited Sheffield to open the new Town Hall. As part of the visit she was driven to Norfolk Park in an open landau though apparently few people had a good view of her because she 'not only wore a veil, but had over her head a black parasol to shield her from the heat of the sun.'[1] Every street along the route was decorated with Venetian masts and bunting. In front of the Norfolk Park gates a floral arch had been erected, there were decorations throughout the park and 50,000 school children had assembled to sing 'Strike Loud Notes of Triumph' for her majesty. According to the local press 'not many children were lost'![2]

'A Gift Worth £60,000'

In May 1909 the 15th Duke of Norfolk announced that he would give Norfolk Park to the City of Sheffield. To commemorate the event a refreshment pavilion was built in 1912 with a stone entrance arch carved with the Duke's image. Although this building has gone the arch still stands and from this spot there are commanding views of the city. Between the 1930s and 1950s various sports facilities were established. Housing expansion in the 1960s changed the park's surroundings dramatically with high-rise estates. Declining resources in the 1980s and 1990s saw the park vandalised and neglected.

A New Lease of Life

In the late 1990s the Friends of Norfolk Heritage Park joined together with Sheffield City Council and other community partners to work on a bid to the Heritage Lottery Fund. An award of £2.4 million was made. Additional money was contributed by other funding organisations bringing the total money for restoration to £4.7 million. The park now boasts a new community building, restored lodges and new playgrounds. An ornate old gas lamp outside the Granville

Living History re-enactments at the annual Sheffield Fayre.

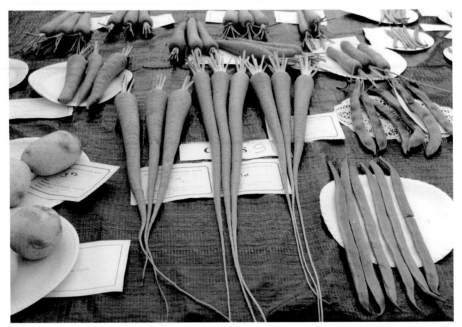

Vegetable entries at the Sheffield Horticultural Show at Sheffield Fayre.

Road entrance has been restored and sports facilities updated. Most importantly the park is used. There is a *Watch* environmental group for 8-14 year olds run by Norfolk Park rangers and Sheffield Wildlife Trust, numerous art and craft workshops, health walks, talks and a whole programme of special events. The most ambitious event is the annual Sheffield Fayre with Living History re-enactments, the Sheffield Horticultural Show, a farmers' market, fun fair, ranger show, classic and vintage car show, music, children's entertainers and magic shows.

THE PORTER VALLEY – ENDCLIFFE PARK, BINGHAM PARK, WHITELEY WOODS AND PORTER CLOUGH

Location: The entrance to Endcliffe Park is at Hunter's Bar on Ecclesall Road (A61) two miles to the south-west of Sheffield city centre. It should be noted that roads have to be crossed at various places: at the far end of Rustlings Road, on Highcliffe Road, on Brookhouse Hill and at Carr Bridge. The only formal car park is at the western end of the Porter Clough on Fulwood Lane where there are also picnic tables. A number of bus routes have stops at or near Hunter's Bar and those wishing to walk down the valley from Fulwood Head can travel up the valley by bus to the *Norfolk Arms* at Ringinglow.

Facilities: Nearly 308 acres of formal parkland and semi-natural landscape along the valley of the Porter Brook, including a three-mile mostly wooded riverside walk along the Porter to the boundary of the Peak National Park at Fulwood Head. The riverside paths (part of the Sheffield Round Walk) are mostly wide and well surfaced, and mostly level except in the Porter Clough. There are cafés and toilets in Endcliffe Park and at Forge Dam.

Special features: Wooded riverside walks; industrial archaeology; monuments and statuary in Endliffe Park (statue of Queen Victoria; Queen Victoria Jubilee obelisk; memorial stone to the crew of the US bomber that crashed in Endcliffe Wood in 1944; sculpture of a frog by Jason Thomson). There is an active friends group – Friends of the Porter Valley (www. portervalley.fsnet.co.uk).

Fifty years of gradual acquisition as public greenspace

The bulk of the park, then known as Endcliffe Woods, was acquired by the Corporation in 1885 and designed by William Goldring, a nationally acclaimed park designer, who kept, as instructed, as much of the semi-natural landscape as possible. In 1888 the town's Jubilee Committee acquired a further nine acres and in 1927 another five acres were presented by Lieutenant-Colonel H K Stephenson. The park included by then, as it does today, a large informal grassed play area, riverside and woodland walks with the added attraction of two former water-powered industrial sites with the ponds (locally called dams) converted in one case into a boating lake and in the other to a refuge for wildfowl.

Bingham Park was gradually acquired between 1911 and 1927, the bulk of the park (eleven acres) being the gift in 1911 of Sir John Bingham, senior partner of Walker & Hall, one of Sheffield's largest cutlery and silversmithing firms. This hillside park incorporates an ancient wood (Trippett Wood) and formal play space including bowling greens, tennis courts and a pitch and putt course.

Whiteley Woods, like Bingham Park and Endcliffe Park, were acquired by the Corporation over a long period of time, between 1897 and 1932, through the Town Trustees and two Sheffield benefactors T Walter Hall and Alderman J G Graves. This

Stepping stones over the Porter in Endcliffe Park.

Stepping Stones, Endcliffe Woods Sheffield.

section of the Porter valley is largely broadleaved woodland and contains four dams, including at the western end Forge Dam.

The final component of the Porter valley sequence of public open greenspace is Porter Clough which gradually climbs through the picturesque Mayfield Valley, an ancient farmed landscape, mostly in Sheffield City Council ownership and up through an impressive stand of beech, ash, sycamore, Scots pine and larch to Fulwood Head. Porter Clough was presented to Sheffield City Council in 1937 by the Graves Trust.[1]

Water-powered industry

The man-made ponds that occur at regular intervals along the eastern two-thirds of Porter Brook within the Porter Valley parks are characteristic features of all of Sheffield's river valleys. At the height of the water-powered stage of Sheffield's industrial development towards the end of the eighteenth century there were 130 water-powered sites on Sheffield's rivers. They occurred on average four times on every mile of river. There are six surviving sites in the Porter Valley parks and the sites of two others have been drained within living memory. These dams mark the sites of metal working workshops. The water wheels drove grindstones for putting a final edge and shine on knives, forks and tools such as saws, sickles and scythes, worked forge hammers or were wire mills.

Such workshops are known to have been in operation in the Porter valley from as early as the mid-sixteenth century. The one recorded at that time (1566), Shepherd Wheel in Whiteley Woods, which is still in a remarkable state of repair, worked until 1930. It was a museum for many years but is now unfortunately closed. The other water-powered workshops had gone out of operation by about 1900 and Forge Dam and Holme Wheel Dam in Endcliffe Park had been converted to boating lakes by about that time. Wire Mill Dam, in Whiteley Woods, was constructed in 1769 by Thomas Boulsover the inventor of Old Sheffield Plate and there is a monument to Boulsover beside the dam.

The usual arrangement for exploiting Sheffield's rivers for water power was that a weir was built to divert water from the river into a reservoir or dam, via a man-made channel called a head goit. The dam was parallel to the river but at a higher level. Water was fed from the dam onto a vertical water-wheel and then flowed away via a tail goit to rejoin the river downstream. All these features can be seen on a walk through the Porter Valley. Sadly some of the dams are leaking and most are beginning to silt up and a major programme of repairs is urgently needed to preserve the industrial archaeology of the valley.

Working conditions in Sheffield's waterside industrial workshops, despite their often semi-rural location, were most unhealthy. There is much striking nineteenth century evidence that grinders in particular were exposed to major health hazards. The main cause of death among grinders was 'grinders' asthma' caused by the inhalation of stone and metal dust. Some grinders ground on dry grindstones and others on wet grindstones. In the 1830s life expectancy among fork grinders, who ground dry, was 28-32 years. Among table-knife grinders, who ground wet, it was 40-50. Some of the danger could be removed by installing fans, but there were other hazards. Grindstones cracked and exploded causing serious injury or death, and eye irritation, sometimes leading to blindness, was a constant threat because of particles of steel in the air.

Water-powered industrial site in a Sheffield valley.

Wildlife

There is a wide variety of habitats along the valley of the Porter Brook within the Porter Valley parks including mown grassland, semi-natural woodlands and plantations, the tree-lined riverside with some veteran trees, the river itself, dams, old walls and hedges and old meadows. As a result wildlife is varied and prolific.

Most native trees and exotic ones occur along the valley, the riverside alders, and the oaks, hollies and rowans in the ancient woodland being most noteworthy. There is also an interesting ground flora. Along the riverside are bistort, brooklime, golden saxifrage, greater spearwort and pendulous sedge. The adjacent woodlands, besides containing carpets of easily recognised species such as wood anemone, bluebell, ramsons and yellow archangel, also contain less well-known species such as bugle, townhall clock and yellow pimpernel.

Among the birds that may be encountered are woodland species such as the resident treecreeper, nuthatch and great spotted woodpecker, and summer migrants such as blackcap, chiffchaff, willow warbler and wood warbler. Along the river dippers, grey wagtails, and the occasional heron and kingfisher may be sighted. On the dams native species such as mallard, tufted duck,

The brook, Whiteley Woods.

moorhen and little grebe can be seen but unfortunately the once common introduced wildfowl, with the exception of the Canada goose, seem to have disappeared. There are also rookeries at Wire Mill Dam and Forge Dam. Evening strollers are likely to encounter bats. In summer pipistrelles and Daubenton's feed over the dams and noctules circle at tree top level.

WESTON PARK

Location: One mile west of Sheffield city centre accessed from Western Bank (A57) and Winter Street.

Facilities: About thirteen acres of open space. Tennis courts.

Special features: Wonderful and rare (though at present ruinous) bandstand – the oldest surviving example in the city. Monuments to Ebenezer Elliott and Godfrey Sykes. The York and Lancaster War Memorial. Impressive gateposts on Western Bank. Stategic location next to the Weston Park Museum, the University of Sheffield and opposite the Children's Hospital.

118

The Creation of a Public Park

The park was created from the grounds of Weston Hall, an early nineteenth century house built by Thomas Harrison, an eminent Sheffield sawmaker. His two daughters inherited the Weston Hall estate on the death of their parents and when they died it was purchased by Sheffield Corporation for £18,000. The grounds were modified for use as a public park by Robert Marnock, who used much of the existing layout to advantage in his design.[1] The hall became Sheffield's first museum (rebuilt in 1935 and currently undergoing major restoration).

Weston Park and Museum were officially opened in September 1875. There was no opening ceremony – the *Sheffield Daily Telegraph* reported that 'Weston Park … was thronged by a well-behaved and highly delighted crowd. The weather was fine. The park looked in its gayest summer dress. The walks were freshly gravelled, the flower beds were trim and well ordered [and] during the day six horse chestnut trees, of the double flowering kind, were planted in the Park.'[2]

Sadly the park has lost a number of interesting features - an iron fountain, a shelter, an observatory, the rustic bridges that spanned the lake and even the beautiful park gates (stolen in 1994). The ironwork and general layout of the lower gateway (next to the University buildings) on Western Bank were designed by Edward Mitchell-Gibbs. The gateway consists of four terracotta pillars with decorative designs by Godfrey Sykes (1803-66) and assembled by his pupil James Gamble. Godfrey Sykes was an

A plan of Weston Park, c 1887.

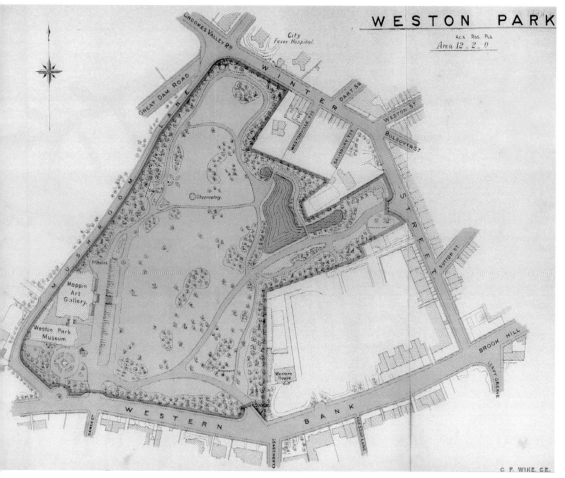

Rustic bridge (now gone) over the lake.

artist and designer who attended and taught at the Sheffield School of Art. The decorations feature designs used in window panels at the V&A Museum in London where Sykes was working at the time of his death. Apparently they were painted white some years ago![3] An obelisk in the park is a memorial to Godfrey Sykes and was designed by James Gamble. It is a made of stone and terracotta with decorations depicting Youth, Maturity and Age, topped by a Corinthian column and a bronze vase. It was erected in the park in 1875. Near the lower gateway is a bronze statue of Ebenezer Elliott (1781-1849) who wrote poems in opposition to the repressive Corn Laws which kept the price of bread artificially high. It was erected by public subscription in 1854 and moved to Weston Park in 1875.

One very special feature in this park is the bandstand – a rare survivor in Sheffield! It was designed in 1875 and built around 1904 with profits from the electric tramway system. The bandstand has been a focus of social events and gatherings such as Whit Sings and concerts for decades. Our hope is that it can be restored and become a focus once again. It is unique in the area.

Another important feature is the lake, once larger and now silted and forlorn. It had two rustic bridges,

The fountain in Weston Park in the days when winters were long and hard.

meandering paths around it with shrubberies and seats and a fountain in its centre. It once boasted a pair of black swans, a pair of mute swans, teal and mallard. However, according to a report in the late 1800s, stupidity is not confined to the present century. Apparently one of the pair of mute swans 'perished in an attempt to swallow a horse-chestnut which an irrepressible boy threw to it for an experiment'![4] Generations of children have enjoyed feeding the ducks and walking along the sinuous pathways.

To the west of Elliott's statue is the York and Lancaster War Memorial unveiled in 1923. It is a massive and evocative memorial to almost 9,000 men who lost their lives in the First World War and over 1,200 of the regiment who died in the Second World War. Alongside is the Boer War Memorial in the form of a bronze screen, transferred to the park from the forecourt of Sheffield Cathedral in 1957.

Again, funding has recently been acquired for restoration work in this strategically located public park. It is vital that historic features are preserved and that the whole park is given a much-needed face-lift.

WENTWORTH CASTLE AND STAINBOROUGH PARK AND GARDENS
Location: Two miles south-west of Barnsley off Lowe Lane, Stainborough.
Ownership: Wentworth Castle and Stainborough Park Heritage Trust. Wentworth Castle houses the Northern College for Residential Adult Education.
Opening times & charges: Details unavailable at the time of going to press because of the major restoration programme. For details contact 01226 731269 or visit the website at www.wentworthcastle.org.
Facilities: Car parking only at the time of going to press.
Special features: Holds a Grade I listing in the English Heritage Register of Parks and Gardens of special historic interest. The gardens care for three National Plant Collections – Rhododendron species, species magnolias, and *Camellia x williamsii*. There are also impressive specimens of sorbus, acer and azalea. Some fine monuments survive in the park, plus a mock castle and a late Victorian conservatory all awaiting restoration. Phase I (2004-2007) of a multi-million pound restoration project is taking place.

A Grade 1 Listed Designed Landscape
Dismissed by Lord Hervey as 'a loquacious, rich, illiterate, cold, tedious, constant haranger in the House of Lords, who spoke neither sense nor English,'[1] Thomas Wentworth (1672-1739), who became the 1st Earl of Strafford of the second creation, and his son, William (1722-1791), were largely responsible for many of the landscape features that survive today. Later owners embellished, added and planted also, thus enabling Wentworth Castle park and gardens to receive a Grade I landscape classification from English Heritage.

Stainborough Hall or Wentworth Castle?
Wentworth Castle is not a castle and it is not at Wentworth, but at Stainborough! So what is the explanation? Stainborough Low(e), possibly an Iron Age earthwork, is the highest point of this south Yorkshire estate. It was the 'stone burgh' or fortification which gave Stainborough its name. Low was derived from the Old English 'hlaw' meaning a hill or burial mound.[2] This mound became the site of an eighteenth century mock castle, but more of this later.

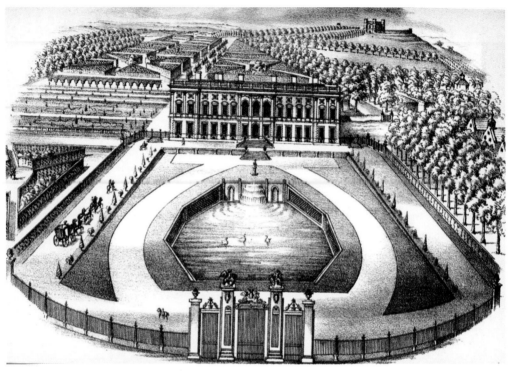

The gardens at Wentworth Castle in 1730.

History of the Estate

In the eleventh century Stainborough was part of the estate of the de Lacy family. By the thirteenth century Stainborough had been acquired by the de Everingham family through marriage and later in that century Adam de Everingham (who died in c 1281) was granted the right of free warren and this family remained at Stainborough for 350 years. In 1610 Francis Everingham sold the manor of 'Stayneburghe and Stayneburghe Lawe and all messuages … mills, woods, commons, quarries, warrens etc' to Thomas Cutler. Between 1670-72 Sir Gervase Cutler (grandson of Thomas) rebuilt Stainborough Hall. This wing (facing north-west), although altered, can be seen today. Due to financial difficulties the Cutler family sold Stainborough to Thomas Wentworth in 1708 for £14,150. He renamed it Wentworth Castle, for reasons that will become obvious, around 1730. The estate remained with this same family (becoming Vernon-Wentworth in 1802) until the house, outbuildings and sixty acres of garden and parkland were sold to Barnsley Education Committee in 1948 for £26,000. The following year it opened as a teachers' training college and in 1978 became Northern College. The Home Farm complex, church, gardens and about 600 acres of parkland are now owned by the Wentworth Castle and Stainborough Park Heritage Trust.

Thomas Wentworth's legacy

From Thomas Wentworth's correspondence it is obvious that he was very keen to purchase Stainborough Hall. One of the reasons was its proximity to Wentworth, and what he regarded as his ancestral home, Wentworth Woodhouse. Thomas Wentworth had been devastated when he did not inherit Wentworth Woodhouse in 1695 from his uncle, William Wentworth (2nd Earl of Strafford of the first creation), who died without issue. He never forgave his cousin, Thomas Watson (who became Thomas Watson-Wentworth when he inherited Wentworth Woodhouse) and called him 'his obnoxious relative.'[3] For the rest of his life Thomas Wentworth strove to have a more impressive estate. By developing his house, park and gardens and erecting monuments he was demonstrating to the whole country, and particularly to his cousin, his wealth, influence, power and political allegiances.

At the time of the purchase Stainborough Hall was said to stand 'very pleasantly upon ye side of a hill' with 'good stables', a park with 'deare' (about fifty deer and nine 'faunes') and a 'sprinkling of trees about ye house.'[4] Once in possession of Stainborough, Thomas Wentworth began to spend large sums of money making improvements 'suitable to his growing dignity and improved circumstances.'[5] His first major expenditure was on a new wing, facing north-east. He chose the architect, Johannes von Bodt, to design this range in the Baroque style. It was said that this would 'make his Great Honour burst with envy and his Little Honour pine and die.'[6] This comment was directed at Thomas Watson-Wentworth and his son at Wentworth Woodhouse. In 1711 Thomas Wentworth achieved another ambition – to become the Earl of Strafford (becoming the 1st Earl of the second creation). Later that year he married a wealthy heiress, Anne Johnson.

The Baroque mansion was finished in the 1720s. The Italianate gardens of the Cutler wing now needed redesigning on a new axis. Thomas Wentworth is thought to have acquired the services of George London, the royal gardener, to assist in this

The mock castle.

task. There are a number of illustrations of the grand scheme that show a series of formal gardens, parterres, lawns, tree-lined avenues and woods intersected by radiating paths. In front of the new wing was a fantastic octagonal pool with a waterfall designed by Thomas Thackwray. It was quite a feat of engineering. A letter of 1714[7] describes the proposal to build a spring-fed reservoir in the cellar of the baroque wing. When water was needed it flowed from the reservoir through a channel to create the cascade. A 'bowlen green' was also made costing £6. There are detailed accounts for painting including costs for painting forty-two buckets 'with my lord's arms' on them.[8] As if that did not impress sufficiently, having been made Knight of the Garter, Thomas Wentworth 'put the Garter on all his shovels, wheelbarrows and pickaxes.'[9]

He increased the stock of deer in the park to 300 and planted Menagerie Wood with a lake and cascade (now gone). In 1728 he set about building a mock castle (now in ruins) on the site of the ancient earthwork at Stainborough Low. There were four towers apparently named after each of his children – William, Anne, Lucy and Harriet. Dramatic views could be enjoyed in all directions and, of course, it could be seen for miles. It is regarded as an early example of romantic medievalism and was inscribed 'Rebuilt by Thomas, Earl of Strafford, in the year 1730.' It survived intact until the early twentieth century. Harriet Piper, a laundry maid at Wentworth Castle from 1909-15, remembered ladies of the Vernon-Wentworth household taking afternoon tea in the mock castle whilst doing their needlework – and being waited on by the butler and housemaids.[10]

During the 1720s and 1730s a number of statues and the building which later became the Gun Room were erected. An Orangery was built in 1728 and a greenhouse was mentioned in 1732. In 1734 Thomas Wentworth built an obelisk dedicated to Queen Anne and his honours in her service – another opportunity to show his affiliations it seems and for self-promotion.[11] John Arnold was head gardener for several decades in the early eighteenth century and was responsible for developing the walled kitchen garden. Correspondence between John Arnold and Thomas Wentworth reveals the variety of fruit and vegetables being grown at Wentworth Castle at this time – apricots, cherries, grapes, peaches, nectarines, pears, plums, figs, lemons, melons and a whole range of vegetables. A good deal of planting and the formation of the grounds also took place under his superintendence. Arnold wrote a poem about Wentworth Castle, some of which is reproduced below:

Of all the places I can name,
Wentworth Castle bears the fame,
Woods, groves, and bowers on every side
For miles, I may say dozens, wide …
Brave herds of deer near to the hall,
Are ready at the keeper's call;
Pleasant cascades below the hill,
Whose flowing streams each bason fill;
From thence with pleasure you may see
Strange birds at the menagerie,
May Strafford, who did all compleat,
Long live to grace this noble sea.[12]

An indication of Thomas Wentworth's desire for prudence and his eye for detail can be gleaned from a set of instructions written in November 1738 to Richard Wardman, his steward.[13] Reference was made to the ice-house which had to 'be filled [on] the first frost' and the digging of 'the two Ha ha's which I design to have dun this winter.' He was concerned that his 'carts, waines [and] wheelbarrows … should be preserved as much as possible' and said 'when the wheelbarrows are worne and uneven they should be rounded by the carpenter' and encased in iron for a longer life. He asked Wardman to watch the sheep for two or three days to make sure that 'they do not spoile the new planted firs' and ensure that 'the great ladders' were laid dry in the barne' so that they would not rot. He wrote at length suggesting that Wardman should devise a long roller 'like a great wheelbarrow, or trough for the gardiners to carry off the grass they mow … and not to spend the whole days work in carrying it off upon their heads in little basketts.' Thomas Wentworth suggested that school children 'one day in a week [should] pick up all the loose stones in ye park' and put them in heaps to be carried away by ass or horse and cart. He also suggested that Wardman and his boy should 'traine up a little ass to draw the daubing sledge [and] sprede and throw about all ye mole hills fresh thrown up, that they may not look ill in ye springe.'

Thomas Wentworth also paid attention to the perimeters of his estate, planting or improving Ivas Wood, Broom Royd and Lowe Woods. In the year of his death he started to build the Rotunda on a knoll at the edge of Ivas Wood. It was said to have been modelled on the Temple of the Sibyl at Tivoli in Rome. The dome rests on fourteen Ionic columns and 'the walls adorned by wreaths of fruit and flowers most exquisitely chiselled in stone; the floor is marble.'[14] It was finished by his son, William, 2nd Earl of Strafford and is presently in a perilous state of disrepair.

William Wentworth's improvements

William was only eighteen when his father died and he spent two of his remaining years as a minor in Italy before coming into his inheritance and marrying a wealthy heiress, Lady Anne Campbell, daughter of the Duke of Argyll and Greenwich. Unlike his father, William never became involved in politics and spent much of his life on his country estate and continued to build, improve and expand. He transformed the formal gardens that his father had so painstakingly constructed. Fashions were changing and the trend was for rolling parkland. Clumps of trees replaced formal avenues. Lakes and serpentines were preferred to geometrical stretches of water. Classical temples and Gothick follies were placed at strategic points to catch the eye. In 1743 William had a marble statue of his father made by Rysbrack. He is depicted in Roman clothing, standing in a haughty pose. This was originally sited in the mock castle but can now be seen at the northern end of the Baroque wing. About the same time the eastern entrance to the estate was marked by a tall stone arch near the *Strafford Arms* and the rear entrance marked by Archer's Hill Gate. He also had a Palladian bridge (originally with ballustrades) built across the three-quarters of a mile long Serpentine. The Serpentine (now silted up) gave the illusion of a winding river. In 1744 William Wentworth had a column erected to his father-in-law, the Duke of Argyll who died in 1743. In 1747 another obelisk was built in honour of Lady Mary Wortley Montagu who had introduced smallpox inoculation into England from Turkey in 1720. The obelisk can be seen below the mock castle and was known as the Sun Monument because it was once surmounted by a bronze disc depicting the

The Palladian front.

The Grade II*
listed conservatory.

sun – 'a device emblematic of the light of reason.'[15] This garden feature is said to be the only eighteenth century monument in the country to celebrate the intellectual achievements of a woman.

Another grand scheme took centre stage between 1759-64 – the building of a new (south-east facing) front in the Palladian style. Just as garden fashions changed so did architectural preferences. The design is thought to be largely William Wentworth's although an unexecuted design by John Platt exists. The rough work was done by Joseph Bower, the estate mason, and his men. John Platt carved the superior masonry including the griffin crest in the pediment. In 1766 a Corinthian temple was built on an eminence overlooking the south lawn. John Platt was commissioned to carve the four columns to match those of the house. This building was restored in 1976. A Gothick Steeple Lodge was built in 1775 and is still lived in. Near the lodge stands a Dutch-style barn with sixteen sandstone pillars. The Home Farm complex may also have been built by William Wentworth in the late eighteenth century.

The Vernon-Wentworths
The 2nd Earl died childless in 1791 and Wentworth Castle eventually passed to Frederick Vernon (his sister's grandson) in 1802. Frederick assumed the surname

Vernon-Wentworth when he inherited the estate. He rebuilt the church in 1835 and was responsible for new greenhouses in the kitchen garden and new plantations on the edge of the estate. Some detailed garden accounts survive for the period from 1878-85.[16] The head gardener was James Batley with a staff of fifteen (including one boy and three women). There was a bothy in which some of the single male gardeners lived and there were regular claims in the accounts for 'soap and candles for the Bothy'. A whole host of vegetables were grown in the kitchen garden including peas, savoys, Brussels sprouts, beans, potatoes, broccoli, celery, cauliflowers, Jerusalem artichokes, onions, spinach, sea kale and turnips. Various fruit trees are mentioned which would have been trained against the whitewashed walls and held in position by 'shreads' and nails – apricots, figs, peaches, apples, pears and cherries – some under glass. Vines were grown – the 'Muscat house' is mentioned and, of course, pineapples. In May 1880 Batley records 'Getting old tan and leaves out, and [putting] fresh into the pit, and plunging the pines.' They also grew currants, gooseberries, strawberries,  melons, tomatoes and cucumbers. Between 22 December 1878 and 6 January 1879 the gardeners were involved in 'putting 300 asparagus roots into [the] forcing pit.' The gardeners were also responsible for the pleasure grounds and chores included 'mowing with scythes and machine', cleaning the Wilderness walks in summer and 'sweeping snow in the Wilderness' in winter, 'cutting dead laurel branches out of bushes', 'tarring holly trees in the Wilderness' and 'pruning the roses in the flower gardens'. Various flowers are mentioned including dahlias, calciolarias, lobellias, carnations, euphorbias, bouvardias, begonias, primulas, cinerarias and 'Roman hyacinths.' In June and July 1882 the staff were 'Potting fuschias and gloxinias'. Some plants were obviously for the glasshouses or the orangery – orange trees, 'cool orchids' from Veitch & Sons, ferns and chrysanthemums. In 1882 an order was placed with Fisher, Son and Sibray from Handsworth for 'Yews, Hollies, Named Rhododendrons, Hardy Azaleas, Andromedas, Kent Peat, Pruning Gloves etc.' amounting to £19 15 6d. Rhododendrons were also purchased from Matlock. The gardeners were responsible for a myriad of other tasks including 'washing plants, glass and woodwork', 'bedding out plants', staking, clipping shrubs, 'catching slugs', 'raking off [the] grass', 'making and painting flower stakes', providing shading by means of canvas or 'shading [the] front of the Conservatory with Buttermilk' and 'shovelling snow and shaking it off bushes'! And of course trying to combat garden pests with insecticide, tobacco cloth, sulphur and soft soap was a never-ending task.

When Frederick died in 1885 his son, Thomas (1831-1902), inherited the estate. The splendid conservatory (a Grade II* listed structure on English Heritage's Buildings at Risk Register) featured on the BBC television programme *Restoration* in 2003.

Evidence suggests that it was constructed in the mid-1880s. It appears to have been purchased from Crompton and Fawkes of Chelmsford. It once housed a variety of exotic plants, orange and lime trees and palm trees as well as mosses, begonias and ferns. There were several pots of *Lilium harrisi* with pure white trumpet-shaped flowers.[17] The cast and wrought iron conservatory is cleverly designed with columns acting as rainwater pipes feeding 'a subterraneous watering system'.[18] The design in the intricate ironwork has a Moorish influence. Originally it was lit by electricity – 'the effect of the light amongst the ferns and flowers, orange trees and foliage being charming.'[19]

In 1897 a further wing was built on the north-west of the Cutler house. When Thomas died he was succeeded by his son, Bruce Vernon-Wentworth (1865-1951). About 1912 he built the terrace that we see today to the front of the Baroque wing and enclosed it with a new stone balustrade. The estate mason, Edwin Bower, whose ancestors had worked on the estate for generations was responsible for this work. There are still splendid views from the terrace though not as impressive as before due to industrialisation, residential developments and the M1.

Annie Whittaker (born 1907) remembers working in the gardens when she was about ten years old during her school holidays.[20] The head gardener then was Mr Thornton. She had to pick the pods from the rhododendrons and azaleas in the Wilderness. If it was raining she had to thin grapes or wash plant pots. She also had to pick potatoes or set potatoes wearing an apron made from washed flour sacks. Her lunch was eaten in the deer sheds and she remembers the deer and Highland cattle in the park. In 1919 Bruce Vernon-Wentworth planted the avenue of lime trees known as Lady Lucy's Walk. It was said that his main interests were his rhododendrons and his pheasants. In 1948, after military occupation during the Second World War, Captain Bruce Vernon- Wentworth, a bachelor, sold Wentworth Castle and about 60 acres of gardens and parkland to Barnsley Education Committee.

The Last Fifty Years

For the next thirty years Wentworth Castle functioned as a teachers' training college and from 1978 it became the Northern College for Residential Adult Education. Barnsley Metropolitan Borough Council managed the gardens extending the collections of rhododendrons, magnolias and camellias which are a magnificent sight between April and June. There was, however, growing concern over the deteriorating state of many important historic landscape features on the estate – temples, obelisks, the mock castle, the serpentine lake, the orangery, the conservatory and other buildings such as the Home Farm complex and the nineteenth century church. In order to secure funding and ensure comprehensive and co-ordinated management of the entire estate, the Wentworth Castle and Stainborough Park Heritage Trust was established. About 600 acres are now under the ownership of the Trust and about £15 million (of which £10.3 million is from the Heritage Lottery Fund) has been secured to enable Phase 1 of a development plan to take place.

A new entrance will be created with car parking in part of the old walled kitchen garden. Another part of this garden will be put back into food production growing vegetables, fruit and herbs used in the eighteenth century. The orangery within this area will also be renovated and re-used. The Home Farm complex, once restored, will provide visitor facilities, student accommodation and exhibition space. The renovated church will have a multi-functional use and may be used for special events, exhibitions or even weddings. Work in the park will include the construction of new paths, some management of the existing woodlands, the renovation of a number of monuments and the planting of clumps of trees in a style similar to that favoured by William Wentworth in the eighteenth century. This will ensure that vistas are once again created and the parkland opened up for visitors to enjoy. Some of the garden area will be cleared and recreated to its eighteenth century design with parterres and formal planting. Another part (on the eighteenth century bowling green) may be redesigned to reflect the garden plan and planting of the late nineteenth century. We look forward to its revival.

WENTWORTH WOODHOUSE, PARK AND GARDENS

Location: Four miles south-east of Barnsley and four miles north-west of Rotherham at the eastern end of Main Street in Wentworth (B6090). The entrance to the gardens is 50 metres down Hague Lane from Main Street and there is a large car park. The entrance to Wentworth Park is 100 metres beyond the Hague Lane junction on Cortworth Lane (B6091). There is limited parking at the park gate.
Ownership: Mixed ownership.
Opening times & charges: The gardens are open 10.00 am to 6.00 pm every day. Entrance is free but a small donation towards their upkeep is requested. The park is open at all times and entrance is free. The mansion is privately owned and visitors must keep to designated paths.
Facilities: Garden centre, café, craft workshops, pet centre, children's play area and open farm. A Farmers' Market is held on the second Sunday of every month.
Special features: Landscaped park with deer, views of the mansion, monuments and lakes. Gardens with borders, knot garden, summer-house, pond, bear pit and remains of statuary. Deer enclosure and short woodland walk. Walls of kitchen garden. Maze planted to mark the Millennium on site of former maze.

Barons, Marquises and Earls
Wentworth Woodhouse and its landscaped park and gardens as we see them today were created largely in the eighteenth and nineteenth centuries by a succession of heads of the aristocratic Wentworth family. The first of these was Thomas Watson-Wentworth (1693-1750) who succeeded to the estate in 1723. Like his father before him (who had succeeded to the estate in 1695 on the death of his childless uncle the 2nd Earl of Strafford) Thomas-Watson Wentworth was an ambitious estate builder. He was created Marquis of Rockingham in 1746. He matched his aristocratic rise with grand building schemes, and the beautification and expansion of his park and surrounding estate.[1] He was succeeded by Charles Watson-Wentworth, 2nd Marquis of Rockingham, who was prime minister twice, dying in office in 1782. The 2nd Marquis was also childless and the estate passed to his nephew the 4th Earl Fitzwilliam and remained in the ownership of an Earl Fitzwilliam until the death of the 10th Earl in 1979.

The Palladian front at Wentworth Woodhouse in an early copper engraving by William Watts, 1779, showing the landscaped park coming right up to the walls of the house.

The mansion

The mansion that can be seen from the park is the East or Palladian Front, based on the restrained classical work of the Renaissance architect Andrea Palladio. It was begun by Thomas Watson-Wentworth's architect Henry Flitcroft, in 1732. But before that he had begun another house in the more florid Baroque style, facing west. This is the West or Baroque Front which cannot be seen from the park. Early in 1732 Thomas Watson-Wentworth gave a party with 1,000 guests to celebrate his son's birthday and the almost completed west facing Baroque mansion, but immediately began work on the east facing mansion, the west facing house being thought to be unfashionable. The outlay was enormous. In 1723 when he inherited the Wentworth estates (which included 90,000 acres in Ireland and country estates in the North Riding of Yorkshire and in Northamptonshire) his yearly income from his estates was £16,000 and this had risen to £19,000 by 1748. And yet as early as 1733 he had laid out more than £27,000 on the building of the West Front and the beginning of the East Front. By the time of his death in 1750 he had spent £90,000 on building at Wentworth.[2] The East Front was still unfinished at his death and work continued on it throughout his son's (the 2nd Marquis) lifetime and, after his death in 1782, his successor, the 4th Earl Fitzwilliam, employed John Carr to make further additions and changes. The East Front is about 183 metres (606 feet) long, the longest country house front in England.

The park landscape

The park is entered through the park gates beside the Octagon Lodge, one of five surviving lodges built in the second half of the eighteenth century at various park entrances. The deer park at Wentworth is the only remaining deer park in South Yorkshire with a herd of about 100 red deer. The visitor is very likely to see the deer grazing among the trees which are scattered about the park.

On the right past the Octagon Lodge and the modern teaching buildings, once occupied by the Lady Mabel College and Sheffield City Polytechnic, is the Stable Block. This building is so stylish and grand that it is sometimes mistaken by first-time visitors for the mansion! It was designed by John Carr of York and built between 1768

A young red deer.

and 1789. It originally housed riding and carriage horses, as well as carriages and coaches, and later motor cars. In the 1891 census thirty stable employees were recorded living in the stables and staff still lived in the stable block until the end of the 1940s. The stable block also contained the estate's muniment room in which estate records stretching back for centuries were stored. These are now in Sheffield Archives. In the latter days of its existence as a college site, the stable block was converted into office and teaching accommodation.

From the park in front of the mansion a high walled rampart can be seen on its southern edge which supports a broad terrace which runs all the way to Hague Lane, providing for the owners what must have been wonderful views to the south towards Derbyshire. In the far distance note two interesting architectural features at the far end of the terrace: a gate house in the form of a Doric Lodge on Hague Lane and a round Ionic temple marking the end of the terrace. The temple contains a statue of Hercules slaying a lion.

Beyond the mansion the deer park, dotted with mature trees, runs away to the east and north with Temple Hill Wood on the right. In the wood at the top of a hill is an eighteenth century Doric temple. Parkland once stretched away to the east and south much more than it does today. By the end of the eighteenth century, following the purchase of Scholes Coppice in 1714, the enclosure of Greasbrough Common in 1728 and the planting of Lady Rockingham's Wood, the park extended from north to south for more than 3.5 kilometres. Land in the eastern and southern parts of the former park is now farmland.

To the north-east, on the edge of the park, in Mausoleum Plantation, can be seen the imposing Rockingham Mausoleum. This memorial is to the 2nd Marquis, a leading whig politician of his age. Rockingham was a strong opponent of Lord North and his government's policy which led Britain into the War of Independence with the American colonies. North's electoral defeat in 1782 brought Rockingham to prime ministerial office for the second time but he died in office during his first year of power. The monument is not a mausoleum in the real sense because the Marquis' body was buried in York Minster. It was built on behalf of the Marquis' nephew, the 4th Earl Fitzwilliam. It was designed by John Carr and completed over a four year period from 1784 to 1788. The ground floor is an enclosed hall containing a life-size marble statue of the Marquis robed as a Roman senator. Around the walls are niches containing busts of his political allies. Outside stand the obelisks that once decorated the ornamental gardens in front of the Baroque west-facing mansion (see Chapter 2). The mausoleum is open to the public on Sunday afternoons during June, July and August each year (entrance fee £1.50) and is entered off Cortworth Lane.

The Mausoleum.

Two more political monuments can be seen from the eastern end of the park in the surrounding countryside. To the north is Hoober Stand and on the southern skyline stands Keppel's Column. Hoober Stand, which is also open to the public on Sunday afternoons from the beginning of June until the end of September, and from the top of which are glorious views of South Yorkshire, was begun in 1747 in honour of King George II and the suppression of the 1745 Jacobite Rebellion. The 1st Marquis' son, Charles, the future 2nd Marquis, had run away during the rebellion and joined the King's army under the Duke of Cumberland. No doubt the monument also enshrined the Marquis' relief at the safe return of his only surviving son and heir. Keppel's Column stands on the former southernmost tip of the estate. The monument, which was begun in 1773, went through at least two changes of design before its completion in 1780. In 1779 the 2nd Marquis decided it should be a monument to his political ally, Admiral Keppel, who had been court-martialled for defeat in a naval battle with the French in 1778 (he was acquitted). The column bulges because it was designed to be 150 feet high instead of the completed 115 feet.

There are three lakes: Morley Pond, Dog Kennel Pond and Mill Dam at the far end of the park. The first mention of the modern lakes in the park, as already pointed out in Chapter 1, occurred in 1739 when the future 1st Marquis of Rockingham recorded that 'a piece of water of three Acres was made to flow from the Terras between Shire Oaks and Old Hague and other lesser Waters for a Serpentine river.'[5] We also know that in 1790, the landscape architect, Humphrey Repton, was at Wentworth planting trees and altering the lakes.

Wentworth Woodhouse Gardens
Records of gardening at Wentworth Woodhouse began as early as Elizabethan times. They are also rich and varied in the eighteenth and nineteenth centuries. The first major feature that we can still see today, the walled kitchen garden, dates from the

1780s. It was in the form of a rectangle about four acres in area surrounded by twelve feet-high walls. This is where today most of the garden centre activity is located. The kitchen garden was typically divided into four quarters by intersecting gravel or cinder paths, with another path all the way round the interior of the walls. To the south of the southern wall was a so-called 'slip garden' taking advantage of the micro-climate below the south-facing wall. This kitchen garden was created in 1786, to take the place of an existing kitchen garden in what is now the deer park to the east of the mansion, under the supervision of John Carr, the York architect, who had recently been involved in the design of a kitchen garden at Nostell Priory. At a later date, early in the nineteenth century, glasshouses were built near the new kitchen garden to replace earlier ones which were also to the east of the mansion.

As pointed out in Chapter 3 the kitchen garden, together with its associated glasshouses and frames, was the source of all vegetables, herbs, fruit, pot plants and cut flowers for the family, servants and guests at the big house on every day of the year. This was achieved either by forcing the produce or delaying its fruit or maturing. At Wentworth Woodhouse the possibility of early maturing and fruiting was enhanced not only by building glasshouses against the walls but also because the north and south kitchen walls were 'hot walls' with internal flues fuelled by furnaces with the hot air escaping through chimneys in the tops of the walls.[4] A close inspection of the walls today still reveals old nails and thousands of old nail holes where fruit trees were trained as fans or espaliers up the walls.

One of the glories of the gardens at Wentworth Woodhouse in the past was the glasshouse complex and the tropical, sub-tropical and Mediterranean plants and vines. As early as the 1740s the 1st Marquis of Rockingham was famed for growing pineapples. He started growing them in 1737 when they were still very scarce in England. By 1740 he recorded that he got their cultivation 'to great perfection' and had produced one that weighed $3\frac{1}{2}$ pounds which was '20 inches in girth the long way round and 16 inches the other.' In 1745 he said some were ripe on 24 March and he had them sent 'to London for an Entertainment'[5] at which a number of leading aristocrats were present (and probably green with envy!). At this time he was cutting more than 200 every year. He was also a successful vine grower, recording that in April 1746 he sent a bunch of Frontiniak grapes and a bunch of Muscadine grapes to the king (George II) to eat 'the Day after He Received the news of the Dukes Victory over The Rebells in Scotland'.[6]

In 1908 all the old glasshouses were demolished and a new large glasshouse complex was erected to the east of the kitchen garden at a total cost of £4,633. This comprised a massive plant house with a central palm and plant corridor 200 feet long with seven subsidiary houses running off to the north and another seven to the south. The subsidiary houses included orchid houses, carnation houses and a fernery. To the north of this very large plant house was a vinery 188 feet long, in a lean-to shape

The central corridor of the glasshouse complex erected in 1908.

against a high brick wall. Behind the high wall and reached from a central passage was a boiler house (with three Senior Robin Hood boilers) and a series of work and storage sheds (a rhubarb house, a potting shed, an office for the head gardener, a grape room and a fruit room).[7] The plant house and vinery were demolished in the 1950s, only the balustraded steps down to the plant house, the high brick wall of the vinery and the storage sheds survived the demolition.

Geoffrey Steer who started work at the gardens as a fourteen year-old in 1936 remembers the work connected with the glasshouses at Wentworth Woodhouse. In winter all the glasshouses had to be scrubbed down – all the woodwork and between the panes of glass. When the vines had been pruned the main stem of each of the vines had to be scrubbed with soft soap to get rid of white bug. The vines, which had their roots outside, were fed on blood from the slaughter house on the Home Farm.

At the eastern end of the kitchen garden a gate opened out on to a central drive which used to lead directly to the Baroque front of the mansion and which in the nineteenth and the first half of the twentieth century had borders planted with bulbs and annuals to make glorious displays edging the wide lawns which gave way to shrubberies and specimen trees. At the south-east corner of the kitchen garden a privet maze was planted in the

early years of the twentieth century. This was uprooted in the 1960s but was replanted in yew to mark the Millennium.

The surviving ornamental gardens lie to the south of the kitchen garden (signposted from the entrance to the garden centre). They incorporate features from the seventeenth to the twentieth century. The gardens are entered through an arched gateway, the gates of which used to bear the invitation 'Come into the garden Maud', placed there by the 7th Earl Fitzwilliam for his Countess of that name who was an enthusiastic gardener. A side-path leads to a sunken 'Japanese' garden designed by Maud. There was a much publicised and heavily visited Japan-British Exhibition at the White City, London, in 1910 which contained two large Japanese gardens. Following the exhibition a number of well-known gardens were created in the Japanese style. Perhaps Maud Fitzwilliam visited the exhibition and came back to Wentworth Woodhouse to instill a Japanese element in the gardens. Although until recently badly neglected, a number of features of a Japanese garden still survive including a pond against a quarry wall with a stone bridge, a cascade, the remains of Japanese stone lanterns and a number of Japanese plants including maples and cherries.

Japanese maple.

This part of the garden, which now contains spreading junipers, rhododendrons, azaleas and a larch seems to have been adapted from a pre-existing fern and rock garden. Beside the pond are the open doorways of a series of duck houses and on the steps leading out of the garden the date of 1868 is inscribed in one of the risers.

To the south of the Japanese garden lies the seventeenth century bear pit and beyond that the eighteenth century Camellia House (not accessible to the public). In that area was the menagerie first mentioned in 1738. In the 1850s there was an amazing variety of birds and mammals from almost every continent. There was a kangaroo (with a 'joey' in its pouch) from Australia, a chimpanzee from Africa, llamas from South America and a brown bear from North America. The lists of birds are equally impressive and include pheasants, cormorants, a golden oriole, a night heron, an eagle owl and a peregrine falcon. At the quarry pond there were pintail, teal, shelduck and a Brent goose. Presumably this is why there are duck houses beside the pond. Not only were there live animals there was also a museum with stuffed birds and animals and mounted skeletons![8]

The Italian garden looking towards Countess Maud's tea house.

To the north of the sunken Japanese garden is a more formal garden, sometimes known as the 'Italian' garden. Dominating this garden, below the slip garden wall in a paved area containing old stone troughs is Countess Maud's tea house covered by an ancient wisteria. Water features form an important part of the garden here. There is a small pond filled with irises and two straight stone-edged canals, the longer of the two running parallel to the slip garden wall, being crossed by two zig-zag bridges. There are some interesting trees in this part of the garden including a large larch and two weeping copper beeches, one of which contains under its sweeping canopy, the statue of a large dog. Stone steps lead up a grassy bank at the western end of the canal to another sunken garden edged with three broad planted terraces which surround a rectangular pond with a fountain. Beyond this sunken garden, leading to a view over the top of the quarry to the pond below, is a series of grassed areas bounded by cut yew hedges.

WORTLEY HALL, PARK AND GARDENS
Location: Six miles south-west of Barnsley. Signposted from the village of Wortley which sits astride the A629.
Ownership: The Labour, Co-operative and Trades Union Movement.
Opening times & charges: All year during daylight hours. Guided tours for groups can be arranged at a cost of £2.00 per person. Phone 01226 2882100.
Facilities: Car parking. Morning coffee, lunches and afternoon teas can be booked.
Special features: Eleven acres of formal Italianate gardens surrounded by fifteen acres of informal Pleasure Grounds. An arboreal delight with giant sequoia, Bhutan

pine, Scots pine, sweet chestnut, beech and an ancient oak believed to be over 400 years old. In Spring there are clumps of snowdrops followed by drifts of daffodils and later by bluebells. There are broad herbaceous borders, clipped yews, a Sunken Garden, balustrades, a pond, an ice-house and rhododendrons galore between April and June. Specialist Plant Fairs are held on the first Sunday in June and the last Sunday in August.

From Wortley village a long sweeping drive takes the visitor past the red brick gardener's house (now a private residence) and a number of one-storey recently-converted cottages (once the potting sheds, store rooms and mushroom house attached to the north-west wall of the walled kitchen garden). The drive then swings to the right to the eastern front of Wortley Hall, now a restaurant, hotel and conference centre organised by and for the Labour, Co-operative and Trades Union movement. There is often ample parking here for visitors.

Some early history

From the mid-twelfth century until the mid-twentieth century the family associated with the hall and its park and gardens was the Wortley family, some of whom were knighted and who, in

The Palladian front of Wortley Hall.

1826, were given the title of the Earls of Wharncliffe. The site of their original manor house is unknown but during the sixteenth century a new hall was built on the site of the present building. This Tudor hall was surrounded by parkland – still known as Wortley Park. The Tudor park had deer and was 'fenced mostly with pales' and had a deer house and fish ponds.[1] It remained a deer park until about 1650.

The Wortleys had another park at nearby Wharncliffe Chase where in 1252 they were granted the right of free warren. Wharncliffe Chase has long been famed for its timbered crags and spectacular views. During the sixteenth century the chase at Wharncliffe was extended and enclosed in a most brutal manner by Sir Thomas Wortley who ejected some freeholders by illegal means and two small settlements were violently depopulated. A number of retaliatory acts followed, from those who had lost land due to the enlargement of the park, involving illegal hunting and breaking down the park pales and walls. These episodes in history have been immortalised in the seventeenth century satirical ballad, *The Dragon of Wantley,* in which the dragon is clearly the lord of Wortley who destroys farms and settlements in Wharncliffe Chase.[2]

A finely-drawn early eighteenth century map in the Wharncliffe Muniments in Sheffield Archives[3] shows the Tudor Wortley Hall, the surrounding parkland and 'Warncliff Chace'. By this time Wortley Hall had fallen into disrepair and rebuilding became necessary. John Platt (1728-1810), the Rotherham mason-architect, was involved in much of the rebuilding of the mansion although he seems to have been preceded by the Venetian Giacomo Leoni who had worked with the Platt family in Cheshire. A 'rough draught' for the south front of Wortley Hall by Signor Leoni in April 1743 can be viewed in Sheffield Archives.[4] In 1758 John Platt was consulted by Edward Wortley Montagu about 'finishing the [east?] wing' at Wortley.[5] He obviously took the commission and appears to have stayed on site for some of the time during construction work because a payment of 4d was made to the steward's wife on 30 June 1758 'for washing the Bed lining for J. Platt for one Month'[6] and this arrangement continued for some time. Platt was involved until about 1790. He began building the west wing in April 1788 – the cost amounting to £860 11s 0d. It appears that further work was done on the east front, the stables, coach houses, granaries and farm buildings if an estimate by Peter Atkinson in 1797 was accepted.[7]

Some landscaping of the grounds took place in 1757 when Thomas Walker was paid for seven days' work for making a vista in High Wood.[8] The following year fish ponds were made in High Wood, payments being made for 'leading stones to wall the pond' and for 'leading clay'[9] presumably for lining the ponds. The first reference to the creation of the landscaped terraces that we see today comes from August 1797 when 'the ground' that was staked out had to be 'dug out to the level of the courtyard' and the soil brought to 'the East front of the house' and 'Clay dug up for the making of 500 thousand good common bricks.'[10] Could these bricks have been for the building of the walls for the kitchen garden? Within this batch of papers are vouchers from the workmen engaged in the landscaping. It was stipulated that the men should be provided with 'proper planks and Barrows' but that they should find 'all other necessary Implements & Tools at their own expense.'[11] The labourers were paid between 7d and 8^1/₂d per cubic yard (we wonder who did the measuring) and one workman, Joshua Hatfield, agreed 'to finish it in a Workmanlike Manner.'[12]

The Nineteenth Century

In 1800 James Archibald Stuart Wortley inherited the Wortley estate and made his first visit to his ancestral home in Yorkshire. Wortley Hall was still unfinished so he stayed at Wharncliffe Lodge, a hunting lodge on Wharncliffe Chase built in 1510 on a hill-top site on the crags. His wife, Lady Caroline Creighton, was expecting their first child so could not join him on that visit. He wrote to her saying 'here I am actually upon the land of my inheritance and am perfectly in raptures with this lodge.'[13] Lady Caroline, who is said to be largely responsible for the creation of the gardens that we see today, visited a year later. The letters to her mother, Lady Erne, exude enthusiasm and delight in her new home and the grounds at Wortley. She said that Wortley Hall, could 'be made very comfortable', and in August 1801 she 'settled with the gardener the place for a greenhouse' and supervised 'the situation of the shrubbery.'[14] The following year she wrote to say 'how altered and improved' everything was and 'the terraces all green, with a great many flowers ... the greenhouse all glazed' and the countryside looking beautiful beyond measure.[15] She referred to the plantation looking 'surprisingly well' with 'very few of the trees dead & since the rain ... almost all [had] made little shoots.'[16] Her mother had obviously asked if she could buy a 'home welcome present' and Lady Caroline asked for 'some cuttings or seeds of some pretty foreign plants which will do well in a hot greenhouse' and suggested Lee & Kennedy as 'the best place to get them at.' In the same letter she said that she had been very busy filling her greenhouse and that Lady Effingham 'had been so good as to give me several plants.'[17] In 1806 she described feeding her Bantam chickens before breakfast and the garden plots in the plantation given to her children in which they 'dig & rake & hoe up the weeds, with some delightful implements their grandmamma gave them.'[18] Thirty years later her enthusiasm had not waned and in her correspondence she mentioned a nursery garden where the profusion of roses delighted her.[19]

The head gardener in the first part of the nineteenth century is said to have been Joseph Harrison who 'launched several gardening periodicals'.[20] Improvements in the garden were still moving apace in the 1850s. In 1853 the 1st Earl of Wharncliffe commissioned Richard Turner of the Hammersmith Iron Works in Dublin to design a magnificent domed conservatory[21] (now demolished, it stood on the edge of the upper lawn overlooking the sunken garden). Turner was the engineer responsible for the glasshouse at Kew. In 1856 the Earl corresponded with Francis Sheilds of London about the statue for the fountain on the south terrace (part of which can still be seen) and the fountain which once operated in the centre of the sunken garden. Sheilds suggested that the latter should be 'rather more ornamental' as less water was available, with water giving 'the appearance of clear Crystal Bars descending at intervals from all round the base of the Figure to the Basin.'[22]

Extract from a letter by Richard Turner showing his design for the domed conservatory.

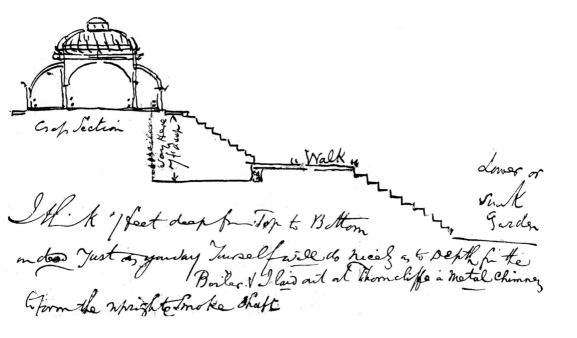

141

An insight into the splendour of the gardens at Wortley Hall in the 1870s comes from an article in the *Journal of Horticulture and Cottage Gardener*.[23] On a dull December day 'one of those pitiless rainy days,' the head gardener, John Simpson, whose 'name was [apparently] a household word' showed the *Journal's* correspondent around the gardens. Simpson became head gardener in 1864 and was still in post in the 1890s. The walled kitchen garden, three acres in extent, was inspected first and the visitor was full of praise for the quality of the produce.

The first glasshouse in the kitchen garden, 130 feet in length, was divided into four sections – three sections contained vines of ten different varieties. In one part were ten year old Muscat of Alexandria grapes which, although they had produced their fruit in early August, still had several bunches of grapes, weighing between three and four pounds each, hanging from the branches. In this range of glass there were also succulents for the summer flower border and azaleas, roses, camellias and lily of the valley. One rose, 'Souvenir d'un Ami', was said to be 'most fragrant' and 'affords a handsome flower for the button-hole nearly every day in the year.' There were further glasshouses, one devoted to other species of grape, in which Mr Simpson is said to have used 'highly stimulating manures.' Another plant house was visited full of cinerarias and bulbs for early flowering; this greenhouse had previously been used for pineapple production. In this area of the garden were borders of 1000 lettuces under glass 'in the highest state of luxuriance.'

A fig house and strawberry house were inspected, with upwards of 1,400 strawberries in pots for forcing. Another span-roofed plant house had semi-double primulas, ericas, crotons, 'daphnes in beautiful bloom' and ferns. There were pits for forcing vegetables in spring and for melons and cucumbers in summer. Winter vegetables that were in evidence included sixteen sorts of broccoli, beet, carrots, salsify and parsnips. The root crops were all covered with leaves to protect them from frost. There were many bush and pyramid apple and pear trees and cherry trees against the west garden wall. For much of the twentieth century the kitchen garden walls were all that remained of this once productive area and until recently the interior was mown grass. The kitchen garden is now part of Heeley City Farm's Food Resource Network. Their plan is to recreate a fully functioning kitchen garden on organic principles. Produce will be sold to the hall's restaurant and at farmers' markets. The small area of old and rare pear varieties will become part of a much larger orchard growing modern and traditional pears and apples.

The next part of the nineteenth century tour took in the pleasure grounds. Against the outside of the south-east wall of the kitchen garden was a herbaceous border 700 feet long and twelve feet wide 'rich in hardy treasures' including *Anemone japonica alba* for autumn flowering. The correspondent described the broad terrace walk, at right angles to the border, backed by hollies and ending with the majestic old oak. The neatly clipped holly hedge and this magnificent oak can still be enjoyed. They then went left through cedars, pines and yews to the terraces in front of the south wing where, on the east, was the 'conservatory with curvilinear roof'. He said that

Veteran sessile oak tree with a circumference of twenty-three feet.

this glasshouse was 'all aglow with chrysanthemums and other bright winter-blooming plants' and was 'a picture of floral loveliness and beauty.' The correspondent also remarked on the 'grace and luxuriance' of the streamers of plants dangling from the roof especially the acacia (mimosa). Finally, they descended the stone steps to the sunken garden with its fountain, rockwork and evergreens.

A Twenty-first Century Garden Tour

From the eastern side of the hall walk across the grass to the stone balustrade and enjoy the views over Wortley Park and beyond. At the southern end of the balustrade notice the carvings of leaves in the stonework (A). Continue south-eastwards with the sunken garden (B) on your right and a ha-ha (C) on the left separating the gardens from the park. About halfway along this path, almost hidden among the trees are the gravestones of three family pets (D). Proceed along the path through the trees which include yew, beech and Scots pine until the enormous old sweet chestnut with its contorted bark is reached (E). Turn south-west, with another stretch of ha-ha on your left, passing a large old beech (F) and huge clumps of rhododendrons. As the path turns west notice the two old oak trees and continue until the pond is reached. In the past this pond not only provided fish but also supplied the household with ice, an important commodity before the age of refrigerators in which to store food and cool wines. The ice was stored in an underground ice-house whose outline can be seen at G. At the northern end of the pond gasp at the size of the magnificent veteran oak tree (H).

From here go along the holly-hedged walk towards the gates of the kitchen garden (I). Here, against the walls, in the open ground and in glasshouses were grown the vegetables, fruit and flowers for the Wortley family, staff and guests. Follow the path, known as the Peace Walk, eastwards and then cross the gardens to the hall and the formal Italianate garden. Walk around this area noting the enormous yew (J) and good views of the south front of the hall. On the eastern side of this garden is the site of the wonderful conservatory that was built in the 1850s (K), with only its undercroft left. Before descending into the sunken garden notice the fossilized tree stump (L) on your right.

YORKSHIRE SCULPTURE PARK, WEST BRETTON
Location: One mile north-west of Jct 38 of the M1 at West Bretton, near Wakefield. Entrance at roundabout on A637.
Ownership: Yorkshire Sculpture Park.
Opening times & charges: Open daily 10am-6pm (5pm in winter). Admission is free. Car parking £3.00 per day.
Facilities: Modern and contemporary sculptures in parkland setting. Yorkshire Sculpture Park Centre with shop, restaurant, toilets, exhibition space and conference facilities. Bothy Shop for purchasing contemporary crafts. Kiosk with souvenirs, ice-cream etc. Electric scooters available free (to book call 01924 830302). The site is hilly. The University of Leeds is currently using the Bretton Hall buildings (with no public access).
Special Features: 500 acre Grade II eighteenth century landscaped park. Camellia House. Good variety of trees including some veteran trees in the old deer park. Fruit-clad walls of the former kitchen garden. Lakes (with restricted access due to nature reserves on the lake edges). Old deer shelter. For further details and events visit the website on www.ysp.co.uk or telephone 01924 830302.

The Wentworth family comes to West Bretton
After the Norman conquest a family named de Bretton settled in the area and through a series of marriages became connected with the family of Dronsfield. From the thirteenth century the Dronsfields began to build up an estate at West Bretton. The last male of the Dronsfield line was Sir William Dronsfield, knighted in 1401. Having no male heir, his sisters Agnes and Isabel became co-heirs.[1] Agnes married John Wentworth and West Bretton came to be owned by the Wentworth family for many generations.

In 1720 Sir William Wentworth married Diana Blackett, a rich heiress from Northumberland. They began to build a new mansion at West Bretton. It was designed by Sir William himself and James Moyser, in the Palladian style.[2] In 1744 Sir William built his own chapel in the park.

When Sir Thomas Wentworth inherited in 1763 he began work on the parkland at West Bretton 'borrowing' Richard Woods, the landscape designer working at Cannon Hall, for John Spencer. This information is gleaned from John Spencer's diary entries. In early 1764 he wrote 'Mr Woods went to Bretton Hall'. In July of the same year he noted that he had 'walked Bretton Park to view improvements.' However, on 15 December 1764, Spencer wrote that 'Sir Thos Wentworth's new Bridge was carried down this day by the Violence of the Flood. Mr Woods generally blamed for his unskillful Directions about the Construction of it.'[3] It is assumed that Mr Woods was relieved of his commission following this incident. Between 1765 and 1770 the Upper Lake was constructed and at some point in the 1770s Sir Thomas decided to have a lower lake dug. Luke Holt, a noted local canal engineer, was apparently given the task.[4] This lake was rebuilt in the 1990s to modern standards to withstand floods.

In 1777 Sir Thomas Wentworth inherited the wealth of a Northumbrian relative, Sir Walter Blackett, and under the terms of his will changed his name to Blackett. Extra income helped developments at West Bretton. Letters and maps give details of a menagerie and a temple on Islands In the upper lake and a grotto or hermitage on the lakeside. By 1780 the Bella Vista was built to the north of the house. This was an amazing three-storey gothic tower with an observation lantern on top (now demolished).[5]

The Beaumont Era

When Sir Thomas died in 1792 his considerable fortune was bequeathed to an illegitimate daughter, Diana, and her husband, Thomas Richard Beaumont. For the next forty years the Bretton estate expanded and the hall was doubled in size. Diana was an obsessive gardener and she died leaving gardens and shrubberies totalling more than thirty acres.[6] In the early nineteenth century Robert Marnock worked at Bretton and was responsible for various garden features including an arbour, statuary and treillage work.[7]

During this period the Archway Lodge was constructed as the main entrance to Bretton Hall. Jeffry Wyatt was employed not only on the hall itself but also to build the Camellia House (much altered later in the century), a whole range of glasshouses, entrance lodges, the bridge over the middle of the two lakes and a large menagerie south of the lower lake. Wyatt was knighted after redesigning Windsor Castle. In 1826 Diana employed Baileys of Holborn to construct a unique domed conservatory

Camellia House.

said to have been 100 feet in diameter and rising to a fluted vent some seventy feet high at a cost of almost £15,000. This onion-shaped conservatory was built from hundreds of slender cast iron ribs and glazed with a huge copper dome. It was considered to be the largest of its kind in the world. Here Diana experimented with her tropical plants. Following her death it was sold for only 520 guineas.

The Beaumonts retained ownership of Bretton Hall until 1948 when Wentworth Henry Canning Beaumont, 2nd Viscount Allendale, sold the hall, lodges, lakes and 260 acres of land to become a teacher training college. The campus is currently part of the University of Leeds.

Henry Moore sculpture in the Old Deer Park.

The Yorkshire Sculpture Park

In 1977 the Yorkshire Sculpture Park was founded to organise temporary exhibitions, with sculptures placed throughout the Bretton Hall estate. The area known as the Old Deer Park has a large collection of sculptures by Henry Moore. On the wooded slopes leading down to the hall are a group of bronzes by Barbara Hepworth and several works by Elizabeth Frink. Among other artists represented are Antony Gormley, Sol LeWitt, Federico Assler, Iqor Mitoraj and Serge Spitzer. To mark the opening of the new Yorkshire Sculpture Centre building in 2002, Gordon Young created a 100 metre long steel pathway, the Walk of Art, at the entrance to the centre. The path is inscribed with the names of subscribers and supporters – a novel idea for fund-raising! The park is worth a visit for anyone interested in historic park landscapes, sculptures or exhibitions. A new exhibition space was under construction in 2004.

$\mathscr{N}$OTES AND REFERENCES

Chapter 1. Parks

1. L M Cantor and J Hatherly, 'The Medieval Parks of England', *Geography*, 64, 1979, pp 71-85.
2. Oliver Rackham, *Ancient Woodland its History, Vegetation and Uses in England*, Edward Arnold, 1980, p 91.
3. Joseph Hunter, *South Yorkshire: the History and Topography of the Deanery of Doncaster*, J B Nichols & Son, 2 Vols, 1828-31.
4. Melvyn Jones, 'Deer in South Yorkshire: An Historical Perspective' in Melvyn Jones, Ian D Rotherham and Andrew J McCarthy (eds) *Deer or the New Woodlands?, The Journal of Practical Ecology and Conservation, Special Publication No 1*, November 1996, pp 11-26.
5. Hunter, *South Yorkshire*, Vol 1, p 309.
6. Alice Rodgers, 'Deer Parks in the Maltby Area' in Melvyn Jones (ed) *Aspects of Rotherham: Discovering Local History, Volume 3*, Wharncliffe Publishing, 1998, p 20.
7. C Drury, 'The Funeral of Francis Talbot, Earl of Shrewsbury at Sheffield, 1560', *The Sheffield Miscellany*, Pt 4, 1897, p 140.
8. John Harrison (1637) *An exact and perfect survey and view of the manor of Sheffield*, transcribed by J G Ronksley, Robert White & Co, 1908, p 3.
9. Daniel Defoe (1727) *A Tour through the Whole Island of Great Britain*, Vol 3, Folio Society edition, 1983, p 59.
10. John Evelyn, *Sylva or a Discourse of Forest-Trees*, 4th edition, 1706, p 230.
11. T Walter Hall, 'Tankersley Old Hall and Fanshawe Gate' in *Incunabula of Sheffield History*, J W Northend, 1937, p 181.
12. John Harrison (1637) *An exact and perfect survey and view of the manor of Sheffield*, transcribed by J G Ronksley, p 48.
13. For a good general discussion of the park in the seventeenth century see Susan Lasdun, *The English Park: Royal, Private & Public*, The Vendome Press, 1992, Chapters 4 and 5.
14. Evelyn, *Sylva*.
15. See Susan Lasdun, *The English Park*, Ch 6, 'The Landscape Park: from Bridgeman to Brown'.
16. Melvyn Jones, ' Rents, Remarks and Observations: The First Marquis of Rockingham's Rent Roll Book' in Melvyn Jones (ed) *Aspects of Rotherham: Discovering Local History*, Wharncliffe Publishing, 1995, pp 113-128.
17. Wentworth Woodhouse Muniments (WWM) in Sheffield Archives, A 1273.
18. WWM A1273.
19. Tom William Beastall, 'Sandbeck Hall and Park' in Melvyn Jones (ed) *Aspects of Rotherham: Discovering Local History*, Wharncliffe Publishing, 1995, p 97.

20. Jill Franklin, 'The Victorian Country House' in G E Mingay (ed) *The Victorian Countryside,* Vol 2, Routledge & Kegan Paul, 1981, pp 399-414.
21. For good general discussions of the Victorian park movement see Hazel Conway, *People's Parks: the Design and Development of Victorian Parks in Britain,* Cambridge University Press, 1991; and Hazel Conway, *Public Parks,* Shire Publications Ltd, 1996.
22. 'Round the Sheffield Parks' by Antaeus, Newspaper cuttings relating to Sheffield, Vol 48, p 127, in Sheffield Central Library, Local Studies Library.
23. Alfred Gatty, *A Life at One Living,* Bell & Sons/ Robert White, 1884, pp 25-26.
24. Heritage Lottery Fund, *Parklife,* 2004.

Chapter 2. The English Ornamental Garden

1. Julia S Berrall, *The Garden: An Illustrated History from Ancient Egypt to the Present Day,* Thames and Hudson, 1966, p 235.
2. Timothy Mowl, *Historic Gardens of Gloucestershire,* Tempus Publishing Ltd, 2002, p 18.
3. The garden is described in detail in Ralph Sutton, *The English Garden,* B T Batsford Ltd, 2nd Edition, revised, 1950, pp 48-50.
4. William Robinson, *The Wild Garden,* John Murray, 1870.
5. Richard Gorer, *The Flower Garden in England,* B T Batsford Ltd, 1975, p 127.
6. Quoted and discussed in Jennifer Davies, *The Victorian Flower Garden,* BBC Books, 1991, pp 35-36.
7. William Sutherland, *Hardy Herbaceous and Alpine Flowers,* William Blackwood & Son, 1871.
8. Jane Brown, *Eminent Gardeners,* Chapter 7, 'Gertrude Jekyll At Home and Abroad', Viking, 1990.
9. Amanda Herries, *Japanese Gardens in Britain,* Shire Publications Ltd, 2001.

Chapter 3. The Country House Kitchen Gardens

1. For good general works on walled kitchen gardens see Jennifer Davies, *The Victorian Kitchen Garden,* BBC Books, 1987; Susan Campbell, *Charleston Kedding: A History of Kitchen Gardening,* Ebury Press, 1996; C Anne Wilson (ed) *The Country House Kitchen Garden 1600-1950,* Sutton Publishing/ National Trust, 1998; Susan Campbell, *Walled Kitchen Gardens,* Shire Publications Ltd, 1999.
2. Robert Thompson, *The Gardener's Assistant,* new edition edited by William Watson, Gresham Publishing Company, 1901, Volume 4, Ch 1, 'Formation of the Fruit and Kitchen Garden', p 4.
3. Joan and Mel Jones, *Wentworth Woodhouse Gardens, an illustrated history,* Green Tree Publications, 2002, p 41.
4. Wentworth Woodhouse Muniments (WWM) in Sheffield Archives, A1475.
5. Spencer Stanhope Muniments in Sheffield Archives 60673/4.
6. Battie-Wrightson Archive in Doncaster Archives, DD/BW/E3/26.
7. Joan and Mel Jones, *Wentworth Woodhouse Gardens,* pp 34-35.
8. Tim Buxbaum, *Icehouses,* Shire Publications Ltd, 1998.
9. WWM A1534.
10. WWM A1389.

The Lodge, Locke Park.

Chapter 4. Visitor Guide
BARNSLEY'S URBAN PUBLIC PARKS
LOCKE PARK

1. Gerald J Alliott, *The Vanishing Relics of Barnsley*, Wharncliffe Publishing Ltd, 1996, p 70.
2. Brian Elliott, *Barnsley's History from the Air, 1926-39*, Wharncliffe Publishing Ltd, 1994, p 80.
3. Brian Elliott, *Barnsley's History from the Air*, p 80.
4. Alliott, *The Vanishing Relics of Barnsley*, p 72.
5. Alliott, *The Vanishing Relics of Barnsley*, p 80.
6. Hazel Conway, *Public Parks*, Shire Publications Ltd, 1996, p 26.

BRODSWORTH HALL GARDENS

1. Caroline Whitworth, *Brodsworth Hall*, English Heritage, 1995, p 1.
2. Whitworth, *Brodsworth Hall*, p 8.
3. Stephen Anderton, *Brodsworth Hall,* English Heritage, 1995, p 31.
4. Anderton, *Brodsworth Hall*, p 33.

CANNON HALL PARK AND GARDENS

1. Joseph Hunter, *South Yorkshire*, Vol. II, 1831, pp 231-232.
2. Diary of John Spencer, 1 January 1759, Spencer Stanhope Muniments, 60633, Sheffield Archives.
3. John Spencer diary, 8 October 1759.
4. John Spencer diary, 11 August 1757.

5. John Spencer diary, 7 April 1760.

6. John Spencer diary, 28 July 1760.

7. John Spencer diary, 17 April 1760.

8. John Spencer diary, 24 September 1760.

9. Spencer Stanhope Muniments, 60673/5.

10. Spencer Stanhope Muniments, 60673/4.

11. Spencer Stanhope Muniments, 60674(6a).

12. Spencer Stanhope Muniments, 60686(25j).

13. Spencer Stanhope Muniments, 60686 (25j).

14. Spencer Stanhope Muniments, 60674/2.

15. John Spencer diary, 3 February 1762.

16. John Spencer diary, 6 March 1762.

17. John Spencer diary, 1 February 1763.

18. John Spencer diary, 26 February 1765.

19. Spencer Stanhope Muniments, 60673/6.

20. John Spencer diary, 30 October 1762.

21. John Spencer diary, 26 February 1764.

22. John Spencer diary, 29 January 1765.

CLUMBER PARK AND WALLED KITCHEN GARDEN

1. Val Foster, *Clumber Park*, The National Trust, 1993, p 5.

2. Foster, *Clumber Park*, p 9.

3. Foster, *Clumber Park*, p 19.

4. Quoted by Neil Porteous in his unpublished *Historical Summary* about Clumber Park.

5. Foster, *Clumber Park*, p 14.

6. *The Kitchen Garden, Clumber Park* information leaflet by the National Trust.

CUSWORTH HALL AND PARK

1. Gordon Smith, *Cusworth Hall and the Battie-Wrightson Family*, Doncaster, 1990, p 5-6.

2. Battie-Wrightson Cusworth papers (DD/BW) Map 165 of Cusworth Hall, Park and adjacent lands 1770s in Doncaster Archives.

3. Smith, *Cusworth Hall*, p 14.

4. DD/BW 113, Volume containing copies of memoranda to Thomas Colia, p 7.

5. DD/BW 113, p 10.

6. DD/BW 113, p 15.

7. DD/BW 113, p 12.

8. DD/BW 113, p 16.

9. DD/BW 113, p 29.

10. Smith, *Cusworth Hall*, p 27.

11. DD/BW/E3/25, Account for trees, shrubs and plants from 1783-88, Perfects purchase, 7 Nov 1785.

DONCASTER'S URBAN PUBLIC PARKS
ELMFIELD PARK

1. Peter Tuffrey in the *Doncaster Star*, 28 August 1996.

2. Cynthia Sharpe, *Elmfield House: The Story So Far*, 1990.

3. Sharpe, *Elmfield House.*

HEXTHORPE FLATTS
1. Frank Pearson, *From a Quarry to a Park, Hexthorpe Flatts Discovery Trail*, The Waterdale Press, 1991, p 1.
2. Pearson, *From a Quarry to a Park*, p 16.
3. Pearson, *From a Quarry to a Park*, p 19.
4. Pearson, *From a Quarry to a Park*, p 27.

FANSHAWE GATE HALL AND GARDENS
1. T. Walter Hall, *Incunabula of Sheffield History*, J W Northen Ltd. Sheffield,1937, reprinted 1973, p 173.
2. Harold Armitage, *Chantrey Land*, Sampson Low, Marston, London, 1910, p 270.
3. Cynthia Ramsden, *A Garden in my Life*, Grafika, Bakewell, 2001, p 16.
4. Ramsden, *A Garden in my Life*, p 85.
5. Ramsden, *A Garden in my Life*, p 94.

HODSOCK PRIORY GARDENS
1-4. *Hodsock Priory* information sheet.

NOSTELL PRIORY PARK, PLEASURE GROUNDS AND GARDENS
1. *Nostell Priory* guidebook, The National Trust, 2001, pp 4-5.
2. George Sheeran, *Landscape Gardens in West Yorkshire, 1680-1880*, Wakefield Historical Publications, 1990, p 35.
3. *Nostell Priory, Historic Landscape Management Plan*, 2000, p 14.
4. *Nostell Priory* guidebook, p 45.
5. *Nostell Priory* guidebook, p 45.
6. *Discover the Park at Nostell Priory*, National Trust leaflet
7. *Nostell Priory* guidebook, p 47.
8. *Nostell Priory, Historic Landscape Management Plan*, p 18.

RENISHAW HALL GARDENS AND PARK
1. Alison Brayshaw, *Yorkshire Gardens Trust* newsletter, Autumn/Winter 2002.
2. David Kesteven, *Renishaw Hall Gardens*, Abbey Advertising, nd, p 4.
3. Kesteven, *Renishaw Hall Gardens*, p 12.

ROTHERHAM'S URBAN PUBLIC PARKS
BOSTON CASTLE AND PARK
1. John Goodchild, 'The Third Earl of Effingham', in Melvyn Jones (ed), *Aspects of Rotherham, Discovering Local History*, Wharncliffe Publishing Ltd, 1995, pp 110-111.
2. Goodchild, 'The Third Earl of Effingham', p 111.
3. *Ivanhoe Review*, Vol.1, 1898, p 123.
4. *Ivanhoe Review*, Vol.1, 1898, p 123.
5. John Guest, *Historic Notices of Rotherham*, Robert White, 1879, p 562.
6. Guest, *Historic Notices*, p 563.
7. *Rotherham Advertiser*, 8 July 1876.
8. *Rotherham Advertiser*, 8 July 1876.
9.Commemorative Weekend booklet by RMB, 1976.
10. *Rotherham Advertiser*, 8 July 1876.
11. *Rotherham Advertiser*, 19 August 1905.

12. *Rotherham Advertiser*, 19 August 1905.
13. *Rotherham Advertiser*, 2 June 1976.
14. *Ivanhoe Review*, Vol.2, 1898, p12.
15. John Henry Cockburn, *Rotherham Lawyers during 350 years*, 1932, p 49.

CLIFTON PARK
1. *Clifton House & Park*, Department of Libraries, Museum and Arts, Rotherham, p 3.
2. *Clifton House & Park*, p 5.
3. *Tithe Map of c.1837* in Rotherham Archives and Local Studies.
4. *Rotherham Advertiser*, 21 February 1891.
5. *South Yorkshire Times*, 26 June 1891.
6. *South Yorkshire Times*, 26 June 1891.
7. *Rotherham Advertiser*, 27 June 1891.
8. *Rotherham Advertiser*, 6 June 1891.
9. Freda Crowder & Dorothy Greene, *Rotherham, its History, Church and Chapel on the Bridge*, S.R. Publishers Ltd. 1971, p 14.
10. *Clifton House & Park*, p 11.
11. Crowder & Greene, *Rotherham, its History, Church and Chapel on the Bridge*, p 14.
12. *Rotherham Advertiser*, 6 June 1891.
13. Jane Furse, *A report on the history of the gardens and parkland of Clifton House*, for Rotherham MBC, 2003.

SHEFFIELD BOTANICAL GARDENS
1. Jan Carder, *The Sheffield Botanical Gardens*,1986, p 6.
2. Jan Carder, *The Sheffield Botanical Gardens*, p 16.
3. W White, *A General History and Description of the West Riding of Yorkshire*, 1837, p 86.
4. *Sheffield Mercury*, 25 June 1836.
5. Karen Platt, 'Sheffield Botanical Gardens' in *Hortus* No 63, Autumn 2002, p 39.
6. Quoted by Carder in *The Sheffield Botanical Gardens*, p 17.
7. Carder, *The Sheffield Botanical Gardens*, p 21.
8. Carder, *The Sheffield Botanical Gardens*, p 29.
9. Carder, *The Sheffield Botanical Gardens*, p 29.

SHEFFIELD'S URBAN PUBLIC PARKS
FIRTH PARK
1. Illuminated scroll to mark the opening of Firth Park, 16 August 1875.
2. *The Graphic*, 21 August 1875, p 171.
3. *The Graphic*, 21 August 1875, p 171.
4. *The Pictorial World*, 21 August 1875, p 424.
5. *Round the Sheffield Parks* by Antaeus in Newspaper Cuttings relating to Sheffield, Vol 48, p 123 in Sheffield Local Studies Library.

HILLSBOROUGH PARK
1. Joan Sewell, *A Strategy for the Heritage Parks & Green Spaces of Sheffield*, Sheffield City Council, 1996, p 65.
2. *Round the Sheffield Parks*, p 127.

THE LIMB VALLEY PARKS
1. Joan Sewell, *A Strategy for the Heritage Parks*, p 173.
2. Sewell, *A Strategy for the Heritage Parks*, p 174.
3. Sewell, *A Strategy for the Heritage Parks*, p 159.

MEERSBROOK PARK
1. Joan Sewell, *A Strategy for the Heritage Parks*, p 57.
2. Minutes of a meeting of Sheffield Town Council, 12 October 1886.
3. *Round the Sheffield Parks*, p 124.

NORFOLK PARK
1. *Sheffield and Rotherham Independent*, 21 May 1897.
2. *Sheffield and Rotherham Independent*, 21 May 1897.

THE PORTER VALLEY PARKS
1. Joan Sewell, *A Strategy for the Heritage Parks*, pp 41-43.

WESTON PARK
1. Joan Sewell, *A Strategy for the Heritage Parks*, p 23.
2. *Sheffield Daily Telegraph*, 7 September 1875.
3. Judy Hague, information leaflet by The Friends of Crookes Valley & Weston Parks.
4. *Round the Sheffield Parks*, p 128.

WENTWORTH CASTLE AND STAINBOROUGH PARKS AND GARDENS
1. David Hey, *Wentworth Castle, A Short History*, English Life Publications Ltd. 1991, p 4.
2. Hey, *Wentworth Castle*, p 2.
3. Joseph Wilkinson, *Worthies, Families and Celebrities of Barnsley and the District*, London, n.d. p 330.
4. Wilkinson, *Worthies*, pp 326-27.
5. Wilkinson, *Worthies*, p 328.
6. Hey, *Wentworth Castle*, p 4.
7. L(oan) D(eposit) 1121, item 180 on microfilm A314 in Sheffield Archives.
8. Quoted by Wilkinson, *Worthies*, p 375.
9. Quoted by Wilkinson, *Worthies*, p 453.
10. Phyllis Crossland, 'Life in Service at Wentworth Castle', in Brian Elliott (ed), *Aspects of Barnsley Vol. 4, Discovering Local History*, Wharncliffe Publishing, 1996, p 26.
11. Michael Charlesworth, 'Elevation and Succession: The representation of Jacobite and Hanoverian politics in the landscape gardens of Wentworth Castle and Wentworth Woodhouse' in *New Arcadian Journal*, No 31/32, 1991, p 24.
12. Quoted by Wilkinson, Worthies, pp 442-43.
13. Wilkinson, *Worthies*, pp 397-401.
14. Wilkinson, *Worthies*, p 419.
15. Charlesworth, *New Arcadian Journal*, p 31.
16. Vernon-Wentworth Muniments: Garden pay sheets and accounts, 1878-85, (VWM 198)
17. Christopher Margrave, 'The Mysterious Origins of the Conservatory at Wentworth Castle', an article for the newsletter of the Friends of Wentworth Castle Gardens

quoting from the *Journal of Horticulture and Cottage Gardener*, 25 August 1887.

18. www.northern.ac.uk page by Steve Jones on the conservatory.

19. Margrave,' The Mysterious Origins of the Conservatory at Wentworth Castle' quoting from *The Electrician*, 8 October 1886.

20. Crossland, 'Life in Service at Wentworth Castle', in Brian Elliott (ed), *Aspects of Barnsley,* Vol 4, p 14.

WENTWORTH WOODHOUSE PARK AND GARDENS

1. Melvyn Jones, 'Rents, Remarks and Observations: The First Marquis of Rockingham's Rent Roll Book' in Melvyn Jones (ed) *Aspects of Rotherham: Discovering Local History*, Wharncliffe Publishing Ltd, 1995, pp 113-128 and Melvyn Jones, 'The Expansion of a Great Landed Estate: The Watson-Wentworth South Yorkshire Estate, 1695-1782' in Melvyn Jones (ed), *Aspects of Rotherham: Discovering Local History*, Vol 3, Wharncliffe Publishing Ltd, 1998, pp 80-98.

2. Wentworth Woodhouse Muniments (WWM), A1273 in Sheffield Archives.

3. WWM A1273.

4. Joan and Mel Jones, *Wentworth Woodhouse Gardens: an illustrated history*, Green Tree Publications, 2002, Chapter 2.

5. WWM A1273.

6. WWM A1273.

7. Joan and Mel Jones, *Wentworth Woodhouse Gardens*, pp 34-35.

8. WWM A1426.

WORTLEY HALL, PARK AND GARDENS

1. David Hey, 'The Parks at Tankersley and Wortley' in *Yorkshire Archaeological Journal*, Vol 47, 1975, p 115.

2. Hey, 'The Parks at Tankersley and Wortley' p 117.

3. Wharncliffe Muniments (WhM) in Sheffield Archives Map 6.

4. WhM 58 (Item 49).

5. Brian Elliott, 'Architects of No Slender Merit: Platt of Rotherham, 1700-1810' in *Aspects of Rotherham,* Vol 3, Melvyn Jones (ed) 1998, p 125.

6. WhM 143.

7. WhM 58 (Item 45).

8. WhM 142.

9. WhM 142.

10. Whm 58 (Item 31).

11. WhM 58 (Item 44).

12. WhM 58 (Item 43)

13. Caroline Grosvenor and Charles Beilby, *The First Lady Wharncliffe and her Family*, Vol 1, Heinemann Ltd, 1927, p 60.

14. WhM 693/231. Letter of 25 August 1801.

15. WhM 693/240. Letter of 8 August 1802.

16. WhM 693/242.

17. WhM 693/247.

18. WhM 693/331.

19. Grosvenor, *The First Lady Wharncliffe and her Family*, Vol 2, pp 261-2.

20. Wortley Hall guidebook nd p 12.
21. WhM 147 (2).
22. WhM 418. Correspondence of 19 August 1856 and 29 September 1856.
23. *Journal of Horticulture and Cottage Gardener*, 22 February 1877.

THE YORKSHIRE SCULPTURE PARK, WEST BRETTON

1. L Bartle, *A Short History of Bretton Hall*, University of Leeds, 2000, p 2.
2. S J Wright, *Bretton, The Beaumonts and a Bureaucracy*, Wakefield Historical Publications, 2001, p 10.
3. Spencer Stanhope Muniments, Sheffield Archives, 60633-17.
4. Wright, *Bretton*, p 25.
5. Sheeran, *Landscape Gardens in West Yorkshire, 1680-1880*, Wakefield Historical Publications, 1990, p 59.
6. Wright, *Bretton*, p 50.
7. Sheeran, *Landscape Gardens*, p 196.

Eighteenth century chapel in the Yorkshire Sculpture Park.

Bretton Hall.

INDEX

Addison, Joseph, 30
Albiston family, 89
Albiston, Henry, 87, 88, 92
alpine garden, 37
Aston deer park, 10

Backhouse nurseries, 37, 44, 108
Bacon, Francis, 29
Bains Report (1972), 24
Barron, Joseph, 56
Barron, William, 22, 53
Battie-Wrightson family, 67-68, 70
Beaumont family, 146-47
Beaumont, Guillaume, 17
bedding system, 35-36
Bingham Park, 115
Bishops' House Museum, 111
Boston Castle & Park, 22, 86-89
Bradgate Park, 86
Bretton deer park, 9
Bretton Hall, 17, 18, 22
Bridgeman, Charles, 17
Brierley deer park, 10
Brodsworth Hall Gardens, 18, 34, 36,
    54-57, 71
Brown, Lancelot 'Capability', 17, 32
Buchanan, Sir Andrew & Lady
    Lucinda, 77-78
Budding, Edward, 38
Burland, John Hugh, 52

Cannon Hall, Park & Gardens, 8, 15,
    17, 18, 40, 41, 43, 44, 45, 46, 47,
    48, 50, 57-71
Carr, John, 57, 133, 134
Casentini, Chevalier, 55
Castle Howard, 17, 48
Castleton, Viscount, 8
Chartist movement, 19
Clifton Park, 22, 38, 90-94
Clumber Park, 41, 46, 47, 48, 49, 50,
    63-66
Compulsory Competitive Tendering,
    24
Conder, Joseph, 38

Conisbrough deer park, 8, 10
country parks, 24
Creighton, Lady Caroline, 140-41
Crompton and Fawkes, 129
Cusworth Hall and Park, 16, 17, 18,
    44, 67-71

deer parks, 7-11
Defoe, Daniel, 8
Domesday Survey, 7
Doncaster, Samuel, 108

Effingham, 3rd Earl of, 86
Elliott, Clarence, 37, 109
Elliott, Ebenezer, 120
Elmfield Park, 72
Elsecar Park, 51
Endcliffe Park, 120
Evelyn, John, 9, 12
Ewing, Juliana, 34

Fanshawe family, 74
Fanshawe Gate Hall & Gardens, 74-76
Farrer, Reginald, 32, 37
ferneries, 34
Firth, Mark, 101
Firth Park, 21, 22, 101-05
Fisher, Son and Sibray, 128
Fitzwilliam, Countess Maud, 136
Fitzwilliam, Earls of, 130, 133, 136
Forge Dam, 25
Forrest, George, 32
Fortune, Robert, 32

Garden City Movement, 22
gardenesque style, 32
Gatty, Alfred, 19-20
giant stride, 24, 87, 103
Guest, John, 87

ha-ha, 15, 16-17, 144
Hampton Court, 12
Harrison, John, 8, 12
herbaceous border, 35, 36-37
Hexthorpe Flatts, 72-74

Hibberd, Shirley, 36
Hillsborough Park, 18, 42, 105-08
Hodsock Priory Gardens, 27, 32, 76-79
Holidays at Home schemes, 22-23
holly hags, 9
Hoober Stand, 16
Hunter, Joseph, 8

ice-houses, 46-47, 144
Italianate gardens, 36, 83, 145

Japanese gardens, 37-38, 136
Jekyll, Gertrude, 32, 37

Kent, William, 17, 32
Keppel, Admiral Augustus, 133
Kimberworth deer park, 10
kitchen gardens, 39-50, 60-61, 64-66,
    107-08, 111, 128, 133-35, 142, 144
Kiveton Park, 12
knot gardens, 28, 29, 30

landscaped parks, 11-18, 132-33
lawnmower, 38
Le Notre, 12, 30
Levens Hall, 17, 30
Limb Valley, 109
Locke, Joseph, 51-52
Locke Park, 22, 23, 51-54
Locke, Pheobe, 51
London, George, 123
London Parks, 18
Loudon, John Claudius, 20, 32, 96

Marnock, Robert, 22, 95-96, 119
Marochetti, Baron, 52
Mary, Queen of Scots, 12, 112
McCreery, Sarah, 53
Meersbrook Park, 110-11
menageries, 82, 136-37
Mitchell-Gibbs, Edward, 119
Moore, Henry, 147

Norfolk, Dukes of, 112-13
Norfolk Park, 20, 26, 112-14

Nostell Priory Park, Pleasure Grounds
    & Gardens, 12, 16, 17, 18, 42, 46

Oxley, Thomas & Scholey, 61

patte d'oie (goose foot), 12
Paxton, Joseph, 20, 22, 73, 95
Perfect, J & G of Pontefract, 44, 60,
    70, 80
picturesque style, 32
pineapple growing, 45-46
Platt, George, 67
Platt, John, 91, 127, 140
Porter Clough, 114-18
Porter Valley, 114-18
Price, Sir Uvedale, 32
public parks, 18-26

Ramsden, John & Cynthia, 74-76
Renishaw Hall Garden & Park, 18,
    34, 83-86
Repton, Humphry, 17, 32, 133
Ripley Castle, 49
Robinson, William, 32, 35, 36
Roche Abbey, 17
Rosehill Victoria Park, 86

Sandbeck Park, 8, 12, 17
Sandford, Brian, 8
Scarbrough, 4th Earl of, 17
Scholes Coppice, 17
Select Committee on Public Walks
    (1833), 20
serpentine river, 15, 16, 67, 71, 126,
    133
Sheffield Botanical Gardens, 19, 20,
    22, 26, 32, 94-99
Sheffield deer park, 8, 9, 10, 11, 12
Shrewsbury, 4th Earl of, 12
Shrewsbury, 5th Earl of, 8
Shrewsbury, 6th Earl of, 112
shrubbery, 34
Sitwell family, 83, 85
slip gardens, 41
Speed, John, 10

Spencer, John, 57-62
Spencer-Stanhope, Walter, 57, 61
Stainborough Hall, 13, 123
Stainborough Park & Gardens *see*
   Wentworth Castle
Steer, Geoffrey, 41-42, 135
Stowe, 17
Sutherland, William, 36
Switzer, Stephen, 80
Sykes, Godfrey, 119-20

Tankersley Park, 8, 10, 12
Tatton Park, 38
Taylor, Benjamin Broomhead,
   95-96
Telford, G & J, of York, 44
Thackwray, Thomas, 124
Thellusson family, 55
Thomson, Jason, 103
Thornbury Castle, 29
Thorpe Salvin, 8
Thrybergh deer park, 10
topiary, 30, 31
Tradescants, 29
Treeton deer park, 10
Turner, Richard, 141

Vanbrugh, Sir John, 17
Vernon-Wentworth family, 127-29

Walker, Joshua, 90-91
Walpole, Horace, 30
water-powered industry, 116-17
Watson-Wentworth, Charles, (2nd
   Marquis of Rockingham), 130, 132
Watson-Wentworth, Thomas, (1st
   Marquis of Rockingham), 15, 30, 130
Welbeck Abbey, 41
Wentworth Castle, 13, 14, 18, 45,
   121-30
Wentworth, Sir Thomas, 145-46
Wentworth, Sir William, 145
Wentworth, Thomas, (1st Earl of
   Strafford of the second creation)
   121-125

Wentworth, William, (2nd Earl of
   Strafford of the second creation)
   121, 126-27
Wentworth Woodhouse, 15, 16, 17,
   18, 28, 29, 38, 41, 42, 44, 46, 47,
   48, 49, 50, 123, 130-38
Weston Park, 22, 118-21
Wharncliffe, Earls of, 139
Whinfell Quarry Gardens, 37, 108-09
Whirlow Brook Park, 109
Whiteley Woods, 25, 114-18
Whittaker, Annie, 129
wilderness, 34, 98
Williams, Don, 98
Wilson, E H 'Chinese', 32
Winn family, 79-81
Winter Garden, 100
woodland gardens, 32
Woods, Richard, 17, 58-62, 68-70,
   145-46
Wortley deer park, 10
Wortley Hall, Park & Gardens, 17,
   18, 31, 39, 41, 42, 46, 48, 50, 138-
   45
Wortley-Montagu, Mary, 126
Wrightson, William, 67

Yorkshire Sculpture Park, 145-47